PRAISE FOR KEVIN ATLAS

"Kevin's ability to overcome adversity is a testament to his character, and I admire his strong spirit and resolve. Kevin's dedicated efforts are setting a fine example for people across America."

GEORGE W. BUSH
President of the United States

"Kevin's remarkable and perfectly told story will make you la

BILL WALTON
Hall of Fame NBA Player

"Kevin is an intriguing subject, smart, affable, and with a dry wit. . . . [His documentary] is a memorable account of an inspiring struggle to finish on top."

NEW YORK TIMES

"Kevin is a true inspiration to the game of basketball."

BOBBY KNIGHT
Hall of Fame Basketball Coach

"Kevin touches every athlete, every businessperson, every parent, everyone. . . . He has overcome more than what ten people combined experience and has come out on top."

TOM SCLAFANI
President of Coaches Choice USA/Select

GET
IN THE
GAME

GET IN THE GAME

Nothing Missing: You Have
Everything Needed to Succeed

KEVIN ATLAS

WORTHY®

New York • Nashville

Worthy
Hachette Book Group
1290 Avenue of the Americas, New York, NY 10104

worthypublishing.com
twitter.com/worthypub

First Trade Paper Edition: February 2020

Worthy is a division of Hachette Book Group, Inc. The Worthy name and logo are trademarks of Hachette Book Group, Inc.

The publisher is not responsible for websites (or their content) that are not owned by the publisher.

Scripture quotation marked MSG is taken from *The Message.* © 1993, 1994, 1995, 1996, 2000, 2001, 2002 by Eugene Peterson. Used by permission of NavPress, Colorado Springs, CO. All rights reserved.

Cover design by Marc Whitaker, MTW Designs.
Print book interior design by Bart Dawson.

Cataloging-in-Publication Data is on file with the Library of Congress.

ISBNs: 978-1-5460-1424-9 (trade paper), 978-1-5460-3695-1 (ebook), 978-1-5491-2418-1 (downloadable audio)

Printed in the United States of America
LSC-C
10 9 8 7 6 5 4 3 2 1

*To those passionately pursuing their dreams
until they become reality.*

*To all whose hearts have not been hardened
by a challenging life.*

*And to those with faith in humanity . . .
may you adapt and overcome!*

CONTENTS

AUTHOR'S NOTE

My name is Kevin Atlas. It's a cool name, right? I actually chose it on my own. I think it's more fitting for a man who has traveled to all fifty states and seven continents except for Antarctica in my first thirty years of life. I'm a globetrotter, a philanthropist, and an entrepreneur, and I've come a long way from being the son of an electrician. No disrespect to my father, Wayne, or to my given name, Laue. I changed my name simply because I've outgrown it. Allow me to explain.

I was a crippled boy in a broken household who couldn't even pass a class until high school. I was diagnosed with ADHD and dyslexia, and I also had a speech impediment. I had to witness *both* of my parents pass away before their time. I wasn't given much in life, so I had to learn, adapt, hustle, and transform.

You see, that kid who faced so much adversity has grown up to become the face of a three-billion-dollar company. That "crippled boy" accomplished his dream of becoming the first D-1 basketball player to play with a disability. That young man with ADHD, dyslexia, and a speech impediment now travels to speak to hundreds of thousands of people around the world as a motivational speaker.

To me, Atlas represented a fresh start, a completely new beginning. I chose it not because I think I can carry the weight of the world on my shoulders but because I am determined to do my part to help. It takes a lot of shoulders to lift up the world and change lives.

My life is truly a rags-to-riches story. I can't deny I am blessed. I can't pretend it was easy. I spent more nights crying myself to sleep than I can count. But through the stress, depression, and defeat, I found happiness.

And that happiness is what I want for you because, simply put, you deserve it. Everyone does. The truth is that most people are too fearful to get out there and work for it. I wrote this book in hopes that I could help you grow from the knowledge I've learned on my own journeys. I want to help you find what you're passionate about. Hopefully, the story of my travels, my challenges, my triumphs, and my failures can inspire you to get off the sidelines of life and get in the game.

—————◯—————

CHAPTER 1

MY CRAZY JOURNEY

"Being aware of your fear is smart. Overcoming it
is the mark of a successful person."

—SETH GODIN

Mom always told me, "Kevin, God has something special planned for you. His favor is resting on your life." But I never really believed her.

My circumstances directly contradicted what she said. It was easier to look at the problems and challenges I was facing than it was to believe that there could ever be a plan or a purpose for my life.

You see, I was born without a left hand or forearm. On Friday, April 13, 1990, as I was making my way into the world, the umbilical cord that had given me life for nine months threatened to strangle that life out of me as it wrapped itself around my unborn neck. I managed to stop it—with my left arm. The cord wrapped so tightly around the arm that it severed it below the elbow, but the loss of that limb also likely saved my life.

Being born into the world under such a grim set of circumstances on a day—Friday the 13th—that so many people have dark suspicions about could've been disheartening to my mother, but she chose a different approach. My mom was a religious lady, and she taught me that the date of my birth actually represented something very unique, very special. April 13—4/13—brought an important Bible verse to her mind that would serve as a daily reminder to me that no matter what challenge I faced in life, I could accomplish all things through faith. It was a verse she would remind me of often. It was a bold and inspiring thought for a young man with a disability. "I can do all things" (Philippians 4:13). The truth I found in this simple verse helped transform my life from something that could have been negative, that could have pulled me down into the depths of depression and despair, into something positive. It helped me embrace the positivity that could turn my greatest challenges into my greatest strengths.

Still, growing up without a left forearm and hand was difficult, to say the least. In addition to the awkward glances at my arm and facing the normal obstacles of everyday life that most people take for granted, like learning to tie my shoes with one hand, I had also reached the unenviable height of five foot ten by the age of ten! My flaming red hair did not help my social situation either. I stood out in the crowd. For most of my early childhood, I was shuffled between the two households of my divorced parents. I loved them both. Both were great people, and both loved me. But for someone struggling to find his way in the world, this constant shuffle just added one more complication.

To say that I harbored a deep grudge against God would be an understatement. (By the way, I don't feel sorry for myself throughout the entire book, just some of the time—so hang in there with me!)

Fortunately for me, I had sports as a way to feel good about myself and enjoy life. I absolutely loved to play sports. At first, I tried soccer. Why not? It's a foul to touch the ball with your hand, so it was a level playing field for me. But remember, I was also a pretty big kid for my age. So I pursued my interest in both football and baseball. Even though I had limitations, when I was out on a sports field, the world and all its problems evaporated in my mind. All that mattered to me in those moments was playing the game.

When I was in seventh grade, a friend of mine decided to

go out for the school basketball team, and he wanted me to try out with him. If you've lived in a cave your entire life and have never watched TV, let me point out something obvious to you: Basketball is a decidedly two-handed sport, and I only have one hand. That's why it came as no surprise to almost everyone else when I was cut from the team.

I, however, was completely stunned.

I didn't make the team? But I was the tallest kid out there, and it wasn't even close! At least I could have made it tough for shorter kids—everyone else—to score close to the basket.

I was devastated.

Until this point in my life, my mother had always encouraged me by telling me that I could do *anything* I set my mind to. I'd played other sports with some degree of success. Why had I been cut from basketball?

I was determined to prove them wrong. And over the next year, I worked my tail off to improve my basketball skills. I used that initial failure as fuel to make the eighth-grade team. I woke up at six in the morning every day to run the block with my neighbor. I spent all my free time shooting baskets at the park, and I joined several basketball club teams over the next summer. I figured I had to work twice as hard to be as skilled as a two-handed player, so that is what I set my mind to do: work twice as hard and get twice as good.

Denying someone with a disability access to normal opportunities in society is obviously against the law. But there are still natural barriers to participating in specialized activities, including sports, for most people, especially people with a disability.

But this is also the part of my story where I stopped feeling defeated by what I didn't have. Being denied the chance to do what I thought I had the potential to do ignited something deep within me. For the first time in my life, I had both a purpose and a passion to succeed. I became the most committed basketball player in the school that year—even if I wasn't on the team.

I'm going to *get in the game*, I told myself. It became my mantra. I'm getting in the game!

My mom stayed up praying for me all night before the eighth-grade tryouts. I'm not being figurative. She literally stayed up all night. Now that's love! And probably also a bit of desperation and worry—she didn't want to see me get hurt again like I had the year before. Apparently, someone was listening to her prayers. When the list of those who made the team was posted, I scanned it from the top to the bottom. I almost gave up, but there it was. My name was listed—at the bottom of the page. I had received the very last spot on the basketball team. I was now officially a basketball player!

I was *in the game*.

As the next several years went by, I continued to pursue my newfound passion for the sport of basketball by joining several AAU traveling teams. Private coaches worked with me to help me master—or at least adapt to—certain aspects of the game that were more difficult because I had only one hand. By the time I was a senior in high school, I was the team captain and MVP.

Now, that is not to say that I didn't have a major advantage as well. When you are approaching being seven feet tall in high school, you don't face many players who can match your height.

But most of the notice given to me was because of my missing arm. I was bombarded with media attention for playing as well as I did with just one hand. I was given a full-page highlight in the Super Bowl edition of *Sports Illustrated*. President George W. Bush saw the article and asked to meet me, so I had the honor of meeting the president of the United States at the San Francisco airport as he stepped off Air Force One. I felt as if I was on top of the world. Little did I know at the time how I was about to be brought back to earth—and hard.

The biggest game we played that season was against Monta Vista High School, the only school in our conference that had a record that challenged our own. The gym was packed with nearly fifteen hundred spectators—including several college scouts who had come to watch me play. Our little high school arena was bursting at the seams. As the clock wound down, we led by two points. But then a guard on Monta Vista hit a three that put us down one point with only six seconds remaining on the clock. It was the kind of nail-biter I had always dreamed of playing in.

Our point guard drove the ball down the court. He shot a layup that bounced off the front rim. As I jumped to dunk it for the win, I was nailed by another player who was going for the ball from the side. On the way down, I landed on my leg the wrong way, causing what I later found out to be a stress fracture in my fibula. The foul put me on the free throw line for a 1-and-1 with 0.3 seconds remaining. Maybe it was the large crowd or the college scouts that I knew were in the gym. Maybe it was the pressure of being down one point with an opportunity to win the biggest game of the season. Maybe it was the throbbing in my fractured leg. But for whatever reason, when I shot the ball, it rolled off the right side of the rim, resulting in a humiliating missed free throw and our team's defeat to our archrival.

Incidentally, there are great players at all levels of basketball, including the NBA, who have missed the front end of a

1-and-1. It's not the end of the world. But at that moment, it sure felt like it.

I hobbled up and down the court for several more games that season until my leg gave out and collapsed beneath me. The pain had been constant since the injury, but painkillers and my stubbornness to admit that I was hurt helped me to show the world I was a tough guy. The stupidity of refusing to admit I was in pain—because that would show weakness and I was intent on proving to myself and to the world how strong I was—just made the injury worse. It was inevitable. My senior season was over. I clunked around school with a crutch and my foot in a boot, feeling like everything I had worked so hard for had been yanked away from me.

Unfortunately—and occasionally humorously—using a crutch for my left leg without a left hand was a bit of a challenge. The pain in my leg I could handle. But the pain of sitting at the end of the bench for the rest of the season, all hopes of playing Division I ball a huge question mark, was devastating.

After years of growth physically, mentally, and spiritually, this setback was the straw that broke the camel's back on my fragile sense of optimism. The next few months were an angry, negative blur even as I prepared to graduate. I was miserable to be around. I was ranting and raving to anyone who crossed my path.

Of course, my story didn't end here. It's obvious, but I still have to say it. The love and support of my mom, some incredible friends, and my faith made all the difference and got me back in the game, even if it was with a temporary limp.

My leg healed in time for a final season of summer ball. It allowed me to redeem some college attention, presenting me with the option of playing D-II basketball at San Francisco State on a partial scholarship. Although the school was great, I felt as if I was settling. My dream was to play Division I. A personal friend, Franklin Martin, recommended I try out for the Fork Union Military Academy. The Academy is a postgraduate school in Virginia that would give me a second chance at a D-I scholarship. It was the right idea for me. I got on a plane to fly to Virginia, and my mental and spiritual healing began to catch up with the healing in my left leg.

The Academy actually isolated me from society, allowing me to spend a lot of personal time to become emotionally and spiritually focused. I had been blessed with a loving family, and I was fortunate to be living a life of freedom. I changed at the Academy from a cynical individual to an optimistic inspirer—the person that I believe I still am today.

I learned there that my life wasn't about my own will; it was all about what I could do to help other people and give back from the blessings I had been given. With the help of Coach

Fletcher Arritt and a healthy dose of patience and perseverance from countless people throughout that time, I received a D-I scholarship to Manhattan College in New York. I was the first player in NCAA D-I history to have a missing limb and receive a full ride basketball scholarship!

I was in the game.

Several weeks after I signed with Manhattan College, a news article ran in the *New York Times* about the scholarship. A Manhattan alumnus called the college's head basketball coach, Barry Rohrssen, to tell him he had seen the article—and it had put him in tears. He went on to explain that his newborn son had been born with just one hand, and since the birth he had felt almost devastated. As a father, he had been looking forward to bonding with his firstborn son by playing catch or going fishing together. Now he wasn't certain what the future held for his child. But when he saw me in the *New York Times* article, he called my new coach to tell him of his newfound joy in his infant son. He had just realized that if a one-handed kid could play basketball at a D-I level, his son was going to be able to do anything. This moment made a huge impression on me.

It made me much more aware of how my perseverance in basketball and in life could have a tremendous effect on others. When I eventually met this alumnus in person, I was at basketball practice. As I was talking to him, I noticed that my shoe was untied, and without thinking, I bent down to tie it. By the time I stood back up, he was weeping. He had noticed that I could tie my shoes with one hand, and he knew his son would one day be able to do the same.

Today, I'm a motivational speaker, and I share my story with hundreds of thousands of students and adults each year—in high school gymnasiums and in corporate meeting rooms. I continue to fight through every obstacle that stands in my way. A one-handed Division I basketball player doesn't make sense. But I'm living proof that anything is possible with the right attitude and the refusal to quit.

The same is true for your life and any situation in which you might find yourself. I'm here to share with you how I did it and the life lessons I picked up to become an optimistic, determined, inspired, and (hopefully for you) inspiring person.

I want you to understand that finding the key to success—no matter what obstacle you face—begins with your commitment to get in the game!

CHAPTER 2

YOUR SURPRISE ADVANTAGE

"What is learned out of necessity is inevitably more powerful than the learning that comes easily."

—MALCOLM GLADWELL

Most of us have something (or some things) that we don't like about ourselves—something that we think is holding us back in life, keeping us from reaching our full potential. It's easy to take a walk down memory lane and tick off the various reasons we aren't where we'd like to be in life.

Have you ever heard yourself saying "If only . . ."?

If only my parents hadn't divorced . . .
If only I hadn't been picked on in grade school . . .

If only I had grown up around successful people . . .

If only I didn't always have to struggle and fight to keep my weight under control . . .

If only I had been raised in a nicer neighborhood . . .

If only I was a little bigger or more athletic . . .

If only I was better looking . . .

If only my family didn't fight all the time . . .

If only my parents hadn't been so strict, had provided more guidance, or weren't so weird . . .

If only I had bought that stock I was interested in before it exploded in price . . .

If only I'd gone to a better high school and gotten into a prestigious university . . .

If only I was better at math, reading, sales, or speaking . . .

If only I hadn't been passed over on that first promotion . . .

If only I hadn't got sick that year, or been born with flat feet, or had a speech impediment, or been so shy and self-conscious . . .

Some of those same reasons might show up on your checklist. You may know some of the same disappointment, discouragement, circumstances, and events that have caused you real pain. But here's the million-dollar question: Are you going to focus on what you don't have and what you aren't, or are you going to embrace what you do have and who you are? That question might seem simplistic, but your answer will have a huge impact on whether you sit on the sidelines or jump into the game of life.

I may be a young man, but I've lived long enough and observed closely enough to know that too many of us at all ages and stages of life are not answering that question in the affirmative. Our focus remains on what we feel we lack rather than all that we actually have.

Be perfectly honest with yourself. What is it that lurks in the back of your mind, keeping you from growing toward your full potential and living the life of your dreams? None of us have arrived at that spot in life where we have achieved all our dreams. If we have, it's time to start dreaming some new ones. But we know when we're stuck. We know when our heart isn't in it. We know when we are just going through the motions. We know when we aren't truly in the game.

Shifting our focus from what's wrong with us to what's wonderful about us sounds oversimplified. It sounds like one more motivational speech. But it's actually a revolutionary shift in focus that transforms our perceived weaknesses into our greatest strengths.

What if I told you that the very thing you think is holding you back could be the key to unlocking your most successful and fulfilling life? What if that physical or mental or environmental disadvantage you disdain, the thing you wish had never happened to you or been given to you, was actually the very best thing that could have happened to you to help you find your purpose and reach your greatest potential in this life?

YOU WERE MEANT TO SOAR!

Stories of people who not only overcame hardships in life but also used those challenges as their catalyst for success touch something deep within the human spirit. Those stories resonate with something inside each of us: *You were meant to overcome this challenge. You were meant to soar!* And when we read the stories of some of our heroes, it gives us hope that we too can turn around our own lives and make our greatest weaknesses work instead to our greatest advantage.

Abraham Lincoln grew up under hardscrabble "frontier" conditions. When he was still a child, his family was forced from their home in Kentucky. His mother died when he was nine years old. He helped support his family by working various odd jobs, but it took him a while to establish himself as a young businessman after having several ventures fail under his supervision.

Full of faith, good will, and idealism—particularly on the

issue of slavery—Lincoln entered politics at a young age but lost a number of elections. Just when he was starting to become successful, Ann Rutledge, who many believe was Lincoln's first love, passed away. He grieved deeply. But Lincoln didn't let his difficult circumstances defeat him. His career epitomized a spirit of perseverance. It's a reminder that even when you start out with no advantages, even when you have setbacks and failures, you have to keep putting one foot in front of the other. The self-educated attorney used his humble background to better relate to the American people. Despite numerous personal and political setbacks, he ultimately achieved the presidency of the United States. He is credited with preserving the United States as a single nation—even through the Civil War. There is a reason he is on Mount Rushmore.

> "Do not let circumstances control you.
> You change your circumstances."
> —Jackie Chan

A fever in infancy left Helen Keller not only deaf in both ears but blind as well. So many of us have heard her story and have grown accustomed to hearing of her accomplishments.

But think about that for a moment: *both* blind *and* deaf! What would you do if that happened to you? With the help of her supportive teacher, Anne Sullivan, Helen Keller not only managed to eke out a life for herself, but she also became the first deaf and blind person in America to graduate from college; furthermore, she leveraged her disabilities into a successful motivational speaking career. She influenced thousands upon thousands of people in her own time, and her story still does to this day. Ultimately, she was asked by the American Foundation for the Blind to be its ambassador to the world, and her so-called disadvantage opened the door for her to meet with kings, queens, and presidents, write books, travel the world, and change millions of lives.

Would we know Helen Keller's name today if the fever hadn't caused her to go blind and deaf? She turned what could have been a devastating diagnosis into the condition that propelled her into her greatest success.

What if I told you that you too could learn to use your "disadvantage"—or what you think of as a disadvantage—to your advantage? What if the very thing you think is holding you back is actually what has the greatest potential to propel you to success?

That is exactly what happened to me.

Today it is easy to see that my abbreviated left arm—my

nub, or my "lucky fin" as I sometimes like to call it—actually allowed me to stand out in the sport of basketball, catapulting me into the spotlight and bringing about many of the amazing opportunities that I have been blessed with in my life. But I didn't always see it this way.

Growing up without a left forearm and hand made even the most trivial of tasks a feat of engineering ingenuity. Think back and try to remember when you learned to tie your own shoes, and that should give you a vivid picture of my toilsome and clumsy childhood! I learned later in college that my brain is actually wired for me to be a left-handed person. Not only was I learning to function with one hand, but it was also the "wrong" hand. Try eating, combing your hair, brushing your teeth, or writing a to-do list with your nondominant hand for a day.

I faced many challenges in my younger years: being the height of a grown man in elementary school (probably with the emotional maturity of someone a year or two younger), having flaming red hair (nothing wrong with red hair, but I already stood out and didn't need one more distinguishing factor to set me apart), shuttling back and forth between the households of two divorced parents, and greatest of all, living with that embarrassing nub. Virtually everything the other kids could do seemed ten times harder for me. Kids tease each other. I get that. But when my classmates made fun of my clumsiness—and occasionally and more specifically, my arm—it was all I could do not to look for a cave to crawl into and hide or explode in rage. Plain and simple, my arm was humiliating to me. Needless to say, I was one angry kid.

I was well on my way to becoming an angry teenager and an angry adult as well.

Thankfully, with the patience, kindness, and wisdom of others, my attitude changed along the way, and I learned to transform my greatest challenge into my greatest opportunity for success. This may sound strange to you, but today I'm proud of my nub. It's a part of who I am, and I couldn't imagine living my life with a more typical arm.

A GAME CHANGER

Playing sports gave me the opportunity to change the way I think about myself. In the midst of all my anger and self-pity, I discovered that other than the missing left arm, my body was actually built to play basketball. I'm nearly seven feet tall, so if I'd been born with two arms, playing this sport would have been a no-brainer for me. Who is going to let a seven-foot-tall guy not give basketball a try? But let's face it—basketball is a two-arm sport: Dribbling, passing, and shooting are all performed through the use of both arms and hands, preferably working together. With some reluctance and a lot of fear, I got in the game anyway. With the help of many special coaches and a lot of practice, I learned how to play at a high level with just one arm. But I still held a grudge, an attitude of *Why me?* that was holding me back until one day when my AAU coach and one of the wonderful mentors in my life, Patrick McKnight, challenged me to look at my circumstances differently. "Kevin, you're looking at that thing all wrong," he told me. "Your nub is not a disadvantage. It's the biggest advantage you've got!"

Coach McKnight was always encouraging me, so I didn't buy into his line of thought right away. I figured he was just trying to make me feel better about my lot in life. But he was incredibly patient, and he explained his reasoning to me over and over. In short, he told me he'd been watching me practice and he'd come to notice two very important things about the nub and its relationship to my body. First of all, the nub is essentially all bone—it's as hard as a rock. And second, while the nub does not look powerful, I am almost freakishly strong on my left side. Combine those two factors, and as Coach McKnight noted, "That thing is a great weapon for a basketball player—and you are the only basketball player who has it!"

My coach was suggesting that the very thing that I had always seen as my biggest weakness was actually my greatest strength. His statement changed my entire perspective, not only on the game of basketball, but in my life too. Where I had been holding back out of self-pity, fear of failure, and anger and depression—those were the very places where I could actually begin to excel.

> "You are responsible for your reality.
> Decide what you want out of the world
> and go make it happen.
> No clarity, no change; no goals, no growth."
> —Brendon Burchard, *The Motivation Manifesto*

After that, I took Coach's advice and began to use my nub to my advantage on the basketball court. It was, quite literally, a game changer. Coach had been right. An "able-bodied" player would typically hold off his opponent with his palm in the opponent's back. I was able to do the same thing, except my opponent would have a rock-hard club digging into his body. Hey, I was just giving other guys a friendly nudge—that's my story and I'm sticking to it—even if a few of my opponents claim it felt like something closer to a punch. Coach began to call this technique "giving the nub." McKnight never coached me to do anything dirty or illegal. But he did remind me to make my presence known to the guy I was playing against. My left arm ends a couple of inches below my elbow. The radius and ulna form the nub, which creates the sensation of two prongs when used forcefully. When I added the nub to my game, opposing players knew I was near.

I sat next to basketball Hall of Famer Kareem Abdul-Jabbar at an awards banquet. He was fascinated that I was able to play at a competitive level with one arm. After dinner, Abdul-Jabbar asked me for a demonstration, so I gave him a nudge. I thought security was going to take me down and have me arrested based on his response. He told me afterward, "The skyhook has nothing on that arm!"

Cal Ripken Jr., baseball's own Iron Man, "took the nub" once too, and his response was, "If you had done that to me when I was playing, I probably would have had to take the next game off."

Abdul-Jabbar and Ripken were being nice to me. Our interactions were good-natured banter. But both men went out of their way to let me know they weren't just humoring me—they got it. My most significant disadvantage had instead become a unique advantage in an arena of life where I had no reason to become a high achiever. If two of the most durable athletes in history were willing to back down after feeling the pain of the nub, you can imagine how quickly my technique worked against the opposing AAU and high school basketball players that I faced on the court. Pretty soon, none of them were eager to get close to me. When they did, they would usually try to fight fire with fire, and they spent a lot of time slapping, chopping, and pushing at the nub, trying to take it out of play. It had the opposite effect. They were the ones who got out of rhythm. For whatever reason, that brand of physical basketball was not very easy for them, even though many of these players were used to fighting for every inch of their position on the court.

> If you can't learn to love yourself,
> don't expect the world to love you back.

Incidentally, when I speak in front of audiences today, I let children come up onstage to hang from the nub as if they are hanging from the low branch on a tree. Sometimes I'll invite adults onstage to try to pull the nub down as I stretch out my arm. Few are successful without extraordinary effort. It's that "freakishly strong left side" that Coach McKnight had noticed!

Participating in sports and giving it my all was a real game changer for me. But that was only the first step in my transformation.

WHO IS THE UNDERDOG?

Let me ask you again:

What if I told you that the very thing you think is holding you back could be the key to unlocking your most success-ful and fulfilling life? What if that physical or mental or environmental disadvantage you disdain, the thing you wish had never happened to you or been given to you, was actually the very best thing that could have happened to you to help you find your purpose and reach your greatest potential in this life?

It was not easy for me to accept the possibility that what I didn't have could be crucial to achieving so much more in life. I'm thankful every day for Coach McKnight's relentless encouragement. Even if you don't have a basketball coach to help you look at life differently, make sure you listen to people who will encourage you to get in the game. Run from those who want you to wallow in self-pity.

Malcolm Gladwell, one of my favorite business authors

and one of the superb motivators of our time, noted the principle of turning disadvantages into advantages in numerous situations in the business world and in everyday life, but the message became a passion for him when he saw it jump out from the pages of one of the most common and iconic stories that has ever been told. Even if you've never personally read the account, you are probably familiar with the story of David and Goliath. If you've ever watched a sporting event on television between a fantastic team and a mediocre team, you might have been told that it is a contest that pits David against Goliath. It's not an even match. It's not a fair fight. The big guy is going to pound the small guy into submission. The underdog doesn't have a chance. The only chance that David has of winning is if there is a miracle.

Gladwell has the gift of looking at the familiar with a fresh perspective. As he read the old story, he understood it in a new way. David, the teenage shepherd boy, wasn't actually the underdog in this fight. It was the heavily armed and well-trained giant who was in trouble. Gladwell proposes that we consider that David's greatest so-called weaknesses—his lack of experience in the armor and weaponry and the battle tactics of his day—were actually his most powerful assets.

As the Bible story goes, the Philistine giant Goliath, rumored to be over nine feet tall, was the champion of a massive army that was threatening utter annihilation to enemy forces. The offer was simple: We'll send out our champion, and you send out your champion. If our champion wins, you turn over your weapons and pay an enormous price, but your army can go home with their lives. If your champion defeats Goliath, we will do the same.

It should come as no surprise that no one wanted to volunteer to fight the giant. They were too terrified to respond to Goliath's call for one warrior to come out and meet him on the battlefield. David, the youngest and smallest of his family, was shocked that not one single warrior in Saul's army was willing to face the giant in a battle of champions. Thus, he ended up being the one man willing to volunteer to face the giant. What makes his act of courage even more incredible is that he refused to wear the heavy armor or carry the impressive sword that the king provided for him. Irritated that he had been left behind to watch sheep while his brothers marched to the battlefield, David faced the giant with the only weapon he was familiar with: a slingshot and five small stones.

At first glance, David's inexperience made him the most unlikely victor in this fight or any other fight. But what David didn't have ended up giving him the upper hand. While Goliath was encumbered on rugged terrain by a heavy shield and a sword, a nimble kid who knew how to throw stones with deadly accuracy from his slingshot brought the Philistine champion to his ruin.

In Malcom Gladwell's book *David and Goliath*, he quotes historian Robert Dohrenwend, who said, "Goliath had as much chance against David as any Bronze Age warrior with a sword would have had against an [opponent] armed with a .45 automatic pistol." As Gladwell so eloquently put it, "Goliath was blind to [David's] approach—and then he was down, too big and slow and blurry-eyed to comprehend the way the tables had been turned."

> "Be who you are, not who you wish you were."
> —Anonymous

Given the option, my guess is most of us would have chosen to go into battle with a sword rather than a slingshot and a small bag of pebbles. Honestly, I would love to have been born with two arms rather than one. Each of us has something we wish wasn't part of our life journey. That's a good thing. No one should wish for problems—they have a way of finding us by themselves. But there comes a simple moment when we need to accept who we are and go out to win with what we have. You aren't going to succeed in life, you aren't going to defeat giants, and you aren't going to get in the game by trying to be anyone other than yourself.

Is it possible you and I have put so much focus on what we don't have that we have lost sight of what we actually do have? Is it possible we have spent so much time trying to be someone we're not that we have failed to be who we are?

WHAT'S YOUR NUB?

The nub is an unusual force, and as Coach McKnight noted, I was the only player in the history of the game of basketball to be "blessed" with one—so none of my opponents knew how to face it. As I've grown and matured, I've come to realize that I have never really been alone, even if it has felt that way at times. Every single person alive has a "nub." Sure, you probably have both your arms. You might not be seven feet tall with bright red hair either. But you've got a nub—that thing that embarrasses you, that thing you feel like you'll never be able to overcome. It's actually the secret passage to your greatest success in life.

Whether you're a teenager, a college student, a corporate executive, a barista, a construction worker, a teacher, or a retiree, you've got a nub. Do you know what it is?

My nub is easy to see on the outside, but yours might

not be as easy to spot. It's the thing that makes you question yourself:

Am I smart enough?
Do other people accept me?
Do I have as much skill or talent as my coworkers?

Or maybe you think you already know the answers, and you're judging yourself:

I'm not as accomplished as my peers.
I'm too shy.
I can't speak in front of other people.
I'm too different; I don't fit in.

Our nubs make us feel less than adequate when we compare ourselves to other people. But each of us has an obstacle; instead of allowing it to hold us back in life, we must use it to propel ourselves forward to greater success and fulfillment.

Don't get me wrong. Not having a left arm presented many challenges that I had to learn to overcome, both in life and in the sport of basketball. So many times, it was far more difficult for me to catch a pass because of my nub. But I was also blessed with opportunities that balanced out those challenges.

I simply had to look for those advantages and then learn to capitalize on them.

This is true of other nubs as well. Many people with disabilities in one area have been given greater strengths in other areas. Blind people often speak of their other senses being heightened. Those with less natural talent often develop a stronger work ethic and better organizational skills. Timid young children can often grow up with a keener understanding of and insight into human behavior.

> Embrace your weaknesses.
> Every flaw. Every perfect imperfection.
> You'll soon find yourself
> not having any weaknesses at all.

Even if your weakness can't be entirely eliminated (mine couldn't!), it can evolve into a strength given to you that no one else has. You are not an accident! Every aspect of your being was created with a specific purpose: to lead you into the great destiny that was planned for your life.

One of the most successful business entrepreneurs in my lifetime is Richard Branson, who has created an array of products and services around his Virgin brand. Did you know that Branson suffers from dyslexia? I certainly didn't until I read this quote from him on his company's website:

My dyslexia may have been an obstacle in my schooling, but I learned to use it to my advantage—turning it into one of the most powerful tools in my bag of business tricks. It's been fundamental in guiding the way we communicate with customers; simplicity, clarity and fun are at the heart of our brand values.

With dyslexia, nothing was simple or clear for Branson in school. Instead of letting that disability—the dreaded nub—defeat him, he let it shape the way he communicated to colleagues and customers alike. I think you are already picking up on this. Your nub has power in and of itself, but the biggest impact it has on you is encouraging you to become all you are meant to be.

YOU CAN DO IT!

In her classic book *On Grief and Grieving*, Elisabeth Kübler-Ross laid out the five stages of grief. You may be familiar with her work, which has been applied to a myriad of life situations.

- Denial—This can't be happening.
- Anger—I can't believe this happened.
- Bargaining—Is there any way I can make it so this didn't/doesn't happen?
- Depression—I don't think I can go on.
- Acceptance—I can go on.

Honest Acceptance

You are where you are, and I can't push you to acceptance, but neither can you. I don't want to do what you must own. Acceptance has its own schedule. Full acceptance probably takes a lifetime. It requires self-assessment and honesty. Honesty may be the best policy, but it can be painful. Acceptance is not saying everything is great and you don't have a nub.

I used to fantasize about having two complete arms. I still do some days. I spent a lot of time in anger, and I still have angry moments that sneak up on me. Because my disadvantage is physical, it was tougher for me to do the mental gymnastics of bargaining. I was forced to make the journey to accepting myself. I had to stop wishing I was someone else and start being who I am. That's a journey we all have to make.

For me, the first step was quite simple. I quit trying to hide my arm. Incidentally, as a seven-foot-tall middle schooler, it is hard to hide anything anyway. So it's not like my efforts were successful. My mentality about my missing limb had to change. I stopped tucking my arm behind books or situating myself so that people would see only my right side. I quit being embarrassed about it. I realized that my arm was the way it was, and being negative about it wasn't going to help me succeed; in fact, negativity was actually making the situation far worse.

One of my personal rules for living is wrapped up in this thought: Embrace your weaknesses. Every flaw. Every perfect imperfection. You will soon find yourself not having any weaknesses at all.

Hustle

After changing my mind-set about my arm, the next step was working hard, so I hustled. Obviously, it's much more difficult to play basketball with only one working hand. But I made up for that with practice, practice, and even more practice. I put in the effort. I followed my coaches' instructions. I practiced longer and harder than everybody else, and I learned the different techniques that would work with my particular set of circumstances. I grew in personal motivation and discipline until it was no longer a matter of busting my butt only when a coach or trainer was watching—it was how I competed, no matter what. I started busting my butt when I was the only person in the gym or weight room. If I didn't win, it wasn't going to be for lack of effort.

No Excuses

Perhaps most important of all, I quit making excuses. If I missed a pass, I quit saying it wasn't my fault because I had a nub instead of an arm. We live in a culture today that is practically obsessed with telling us it's okay to blame others for the problems we face instead of taking responsibility for our own choices and actions. That's a recipe for failure.

I could have sat back and blamed any number of things for my disadvantages in life and on the court. As I noted earlier, I wallowed in self-pity and excuses during the dark seasons of my life. I'll tell you straight-up: That doesn't work. When I took charge of my nub, my attitude, and my life, things really began to change.

But Kevin, isn't there a difference between making excuses and "explaining things"?

I'm sure there is a difference between understanding why things go wrong and making excuses. I'm not trying to be harsh or dogmatic. As a competitive athlete, I know you don't win every game. You don't make every sale. You don't get an A on every paper—at least most of us don't. You don't always get the date. Not every business deal works out.

At the heart of excuse making is the belief that we aren't responsible. I think it is a defensive reaction so that we won't feel bad about ourselves. But I'd argue that it does the opposite. Excuses don't make us stronger; they actually make us weaker because excuses let us be a passive participant in our life rather than a star player in the game.

I have discovered that when I make excuses, I stop learning, I stop making goals, and I stop listening to the quiet voice of my dreams and aspirations. I stop believing in myself enough to hold myself accountable; I stop competing in the game and instead slink into life's stands as a spectator.

Embrace Who You Are

Just like Coach McKnight taught me many years ago out on the basketball court, I want to first challenge you to accept your nub. But then I want you to take it a step further and embrace your nub! Find a way to make your nub work for you.

I was born with a nub instead of a working left arm. That does not make me a freak, a mistake, or a second-class citizen. I personally believe I was created with a wonderful purpose and future in life. I believe you are too, even though you might have a nub of your own. Nothing is holding you back in life. You already have everything you need to achieve your greatest level of success.

What do the voices inside your head say to you? That you're too young? Too old? Too much of a failure? Too poor? Too uneducated? Too inadequate in whatever way?

I want you to change the way you think! Begin to see those very things as your *greatest* advantage. History is full of stories of people who refused to accept their limitations. And those are the stories that we remember and pass on to future generations.

> What if the very thing you think
> is holding you back is actually what has
> the greatest potential to propel you to success?

Derrick Coleman, deaf since the age of three, went on to become a fullback for the Seattle Seahawks despite those who said it could never be done. In his words, "They told me it couldn't be done, that I was a lost cause. I was picked on and picked last. Coaches didn't know how to talk to me. They gave up on me. Told me I should just quit. They didn't call my name. Told me it was over. But I've been deaf since I was three, so I didn't listen."

Did you catch that? He was deaf, so he did not listen to

those who said, "You can't." His hearing loss allowed him to be able to concentrate on his game by tuning out the crowd noise more than hearing players ever could. He has turned what could have been his greatest weakness into a huge asset.

WHAT DOES SUCCESS MEAN TO YOU?

Along those lines, it's important to realize that success is going to look different for each one of us. I believe that's because each of us has been created one of a kind with gifts that are not identical with the talents of anyone else on the face of this earth. I believe *you* are here for a reason. And your greatest success will involve finding and fulfilling that purpose for your life.

Let me say that a different way: True success has nothing to do with money. It has nothing to do with position or power. It has everything to do with being faithful to your purpose, calling, passion, and core values.

You could be the CEO of a multimillion-dollar company and still be a complete failure at what really matters in life. Or you could be a teacher, a small business owner, a bus driver, or a minister and be the greatest success that the world has ever seen.

I'm like most red-blooded Americans. I like to make money. But I can honestly say when I take time each year to set goals and make plans for the next twelve months, I've never written down dollar signs as part of what I want to accomplish. Maybe I should. And there's nothing wrong with wanting to increase revenue. But when I think about what will make a year successful, it is always about the number of lives I get to touch through my speaking and writing. It's a bit like happiness. People who make happiness their goal often struggle the most to find it. Happiness is a by-product of living a meaningful life. In the same way, make sure your definition of success is about having a purpose and making a positive difference in your world.

When was the last time you wrote down a list of goals? When was the last time you asked yourself what you would consider a successful life to look like?

SEIZE THE DAY!

Most of us have seen the movie *Dead Poets Society* in which a teacher changes the lives of his students by teaching them the concept of *carpe diem*, which in Latin means to "seize the day." This phrase was originally used in the writing of the ancient Roman poet Horace to express the idea that we need to enjoy life while we can because we aren't promised tomorrow; therefore, we should seize *this* day, *this* moment that we have in our hands and make it count.

From ancient times all the way up to our day, people have known that they need to push through the obstacles that confront them and move forward with life, making every moment count. Have you ever noticed how people who made a difference that has lasted for years, decades, or even centuries understood the importance of living in the moment?

Mahatma Gandhi, the man who peacefully brought independence to India, said, "Live as if you were to die tomorrow. Learn as if you were to live forever." Mother Teresa, the mother to the orphans of Calcutta, said, "Yesterday is gone. Tomorrow has not yet come. We have only today. Let us begin." The beloved poet and thinker Henry David Thoreau said, "You must live in the present, launch yourself on every wave, find your eternity in each moment. Fools stand on their island of opportunities and look toward another land. There is no other land; there is no other life but this." Eckhart Tolle, writer on spirituality, said, "Realize deeply that the present moment is all you have. Make the NOW the primary focus of your life."

It's hard to miss the theme that today is the day . . . my day . . . your day! In other words, grab the day in which you are living for all that it is worth. Don't let anything—especially not a nub of any kind—hold you back.

What's your nub? Whatever it is, let it revolutionize your

life. Don't hide it in secret any longer in embarrassment or shame. Bring it out into the light of acceptance and allow it to transform your life. That's when you will get in the game and stop being a spectator.

FOR FURTHER REFLECTION

What's your "nub"? What challenges are you working to overcome today? It may not be as obvious to others as my missing left arm, but it can be just as detrimental to your life if you do not deal with it head-on.

Try to think outside the box. How might you reframe your nub in your mind as your greatest opportunity rather than your greatest obstacle? How can you begin to look at it in a different light?

One of the greatest keys to turning a nub into an advantage is knowing where to put your focus. What are you focusing on? How can you change your focus to motivate you to achieve greater levels of success?

Nubs can be painful to face. They can be incredibly challenging to overcome. But they can also be the greatest catalyst for personal growth that you will ever have. What lessons have you learned from your nub that you might not have learned in any other way? How can those lessons be used to transform your life and the lives of other people?

CHAPTER 3

THE POWER OF GOOD HABITS

"People do not decide their futures; they decide their habits and their habits decide their futures."

—F. M. ALEXANDER

Mark Cuban is an American billionaire who became rich by building and selling the tech company Broadcast.com. He became a household name as owner of the NBA's Dallas Mavericks and lead investor on the long-running and very popular TV show *Shark Tank*. In an interview, he was asked about the secret of his success. Many of us suspect that the quickest way to success and wealth is starting out with money or asking our personal connections to help set us up with lucrative deals.

Not Mark Cuban.

To him, those "obvious" foundations to success are not actually the case. "It's not about money or connections," he said. "It's the willingness to outwork and outlearn everyone."

Most currently successful people did not become that way because of what they started out with—whether it be money, connections, or even a prestigious education. If that were the case, lottery winners would be more likely to become successful after they banked their winnings. But did you know that the average lottery winner is far more likely to *declare bankruptcy* within three to five years than the average American?

Lottery winners—declaring bankruptcy? How could that be possible?

Not just that, but studies have shown that winning the lottery makes most people less happy and healthy than they were before.

In the *Washington Post* article "How Not to Squander the $1.5 Billion Powerball Jackpot," Jonnelle Marte wrote, "Evidence shows that most people who make it to the top one percent of income earners usually don't stay at the top for very long." Many lottery winners struggle with depression, divorce, and suicide. The ones who do survive the lottery windfall and thrive afterward are the ones who—get this—*do not change their daily lives!*

It seems that practicing good habits like frugality, self-discipline, hard work, and delayed gratification makes the difference to any kind of success in life even if boatloads of money are handed to you just for picking a lucky string of numbers!

Purpose and hard work will fill your journey
with passion.

One lottery winner from Missouri managed to thrive after splitting a $224 million Powerball jackpot with her coworkers, but it wasn't easy. Her words are important for us to hear if we want to learn how to truly have success in life: "I know a lot of people who won the lottery and are broke today," she says. "If you're not disciplined, you will go broke. I don't care how much money you have."

Habits.

Discipline.

Stick-to-it-iveness.

Whatever you want to call it, it's the "stuff" that will either make you or break you in this life.

I talk to young people countless times each year as a speaker. I'm not one of those guys who exits out the back door as fast as

I can after the speech. (It's also difficult to sneak out of any-where when you are nearly seven feet tall.) I want to interact with members of my audience and listen to what is going on with them. I have a good listening ear, and I know that many people of all ages and from all walks of life struggle with feel-ings of being unheard or unregarded. Some of my best insights and encouragement have come from just being there for them. Unsurprisingly, many young people feel like they have a limited future because they believe they are already so far behind the high achievers. One of the hardest messages to convey to people is that nothing is truly out of reach. While not all of us are going to be professional athletes or billionaire savants, I believe with all my heart that we can all accom-plish way more than we think possible by simply getting in the game.

I think that's what Mark Cuban was saying: "Outwork and outlearn" others. That's putting yourself on center court in the game of life.

YOU WILL NEVER "ARRIVE"— IT'S A JOURNEY!

Do you have the idea, maybe in the back of your mind, that someday you will finally reach that magical place called "suc-cess"? Maybe it's the idea that you will finally have all the money you will ever need and own a big house and a fast car; maybe you will land the job you've always dreamed about or graduate from the college of your dreams; maybe you will be drafted as a professional in whatever sport you happen to play.

What I've learned in my few short years on earth is that success is a journey. It's not about arriving somewhere. It's about doing things with excellence so that even as we reach our goals, we have already established new benchmarks that are defined by our ever-expanding purpose.

Contentment has a place in life. We need to enjoy and appreciate what we have right now. We need to savor every moment of life. But as we work, learn, and grow, it is healthy to aspire to have a bigger impact on the world.

If success is a journey, we need to realize that there is no dot on the map called "success"; it isn't a destination. The secret is finding the balance of contentment and aspiration. We do that by understanding our purpose and setting our goals. Some people preach that you should follow your passion. My belief is that when you know your purpose and set goals to fulfilling it, the passion will follow.

One way to keep yourself from being limited by a destination mind-set is understanding how to set goals. There are short-term goals and long-term goals. Your long-term goals need to be less specific and much more purpose driven. Your short-term goals, on the other hand, should be much more specific and task driven.

What if you determined that your life would be successful once you achieved a particular promotion or financial threshold? What would you do if you got there in the next few years? Would you say that your life's purpose has been fulfilled? You would be bored to tears!

Having a purpose that you attempt to fulfill through a series of short-term and long-term goals is what will allow you to want more, expect more, and strive for more without living in a state of dissatisfaction in which you are miserable to be around, especially to yourself.

Alexander the Great, who earned the title of "Great" because of his military prowess, died a broken man. Why? Deep in the Hindu Kush, his soldiers finally refused to follow him forward to conquer what was beyond yet another mountain. It's said that he, at a young age, forced to begin the journey home, looked to the east and wept "salt tears" because there were no more worlds to conquer. He literally ran out of countries to conquer! It is ironic that the man whose armies couldn't be conquered was defeated by simply no longer having a greater purpose. As brilliant and talented as he was, Alexander had a huge blind spot. He didn't understand how to renew his purpose in life.

St. Paul is a man whose name appears on schools and hospitals all over the world. He is the author of several letters that make up books of the Bible. No historian would question that he was driven by purpose. He traveled throughout the land surrounding the Mediterranean Sea to spread a message of forgiveness, healing, reconciliation, and hope. His goal was to reach the whole world with his message. He accomplished all he did because he was driven by his purpose. In his own words he wrote: "So let's keep focused on that goal. . . . Now that we're on the right track, let's stay on it" (Philippians 3:15–16 MSG).

> "If you're not getting the results you want in life,
> the first place to look is your daily habits and routines."
> **—Anonymous**

It is purpose that gives life meaning. When we stay on that track with discipline and diligence, the journey becomes filled with joy even on the difficult and bumpy roads.

Get in the game, but realize you won't ever reach a final destination. If you win the championship this year, a new season awaits you a few months later. Get used to living life on the road. One foot in front of the other. Another hill to climb.

Another river to cross. New people to meet: some friends and some who would tear you down. It doesn't matter; you are on the journey of a lifetime!

We must always keep striving, keep reaching for our goals, keep pushing forward and working hard to meet our highest potential.

WORK IS GOOD FOR YOU!

Have you ever had the Monday morning blues? It's tempting to want to complain about having to go to work—but when you really think about it, if you aren't working, what would you be doing? Sleeping all day? Binge-watching Netflix? Wondering how to make the house payment? Think about it. Work may be hard, but it sure beats the alternative!

The truth is, I believe that we were created to work. I don't think that work was ever meant to be drudgery—it was meant to be a fulfilling part of our lives. Having no purpose other than self-gratification is bad for human beings. Not working at a task or having no purpose or no reason to get out of bed in the morning is bad for people. Not following a routine or not practicing daily habits is terrible. Scientists have actually discovered that work is good for your health. Whether you are paid or not, work is important for your well-being. Learn to enjoy it and to use it for your maximum benefit. Work contributes to our happiness, it helps us to build confidence in our skills, it boosts our self-esteem, and it provides us with financial rewards. It keeps us busy and challenges our minds and our bodies to achieve more and be better than we were the day before.

We can develop our talents, cultivate a sense of pride in our accomplishments, discover our true identity, and strive for personal achievements. We socialize at our workplaces, make friends, build contacts, and receive emotional support for the challenges of life. And work is the means by which the vast majority of us secure an income to support ourselves and explore our interests and hobbies.

If we didn't work, what would we do? Who would we be?

In 2006, the Department for Work and Pensions published an independent review of the relationship between work, health, and the consequences suffered when people are out of work. Here's a summary of what they found:

People who have positive, challenging work to do each day tend to enjoy happier and healthier lives than those who do not have these opportunities. Our physical and mental health is generally improved through work. When we are able to work, we recover from illnesses more quickly and we are at a significantly lower risk of long-term disease or incapacitation. Because of these amazing benefits of work, it is important that sick and disabled people either remain in their work or return to it as soon as their health conditions permit.

People who have been injured or who suffer from chronic illness and therefore cannot work are significantly and negatively affected by their situation in many ways. Being out of work is not only financially crippling, but it can also cause social isolation, depression, anxiety, and other mental and emotional issues. People who are unemployed have vastly higher rates of physical and mental health problems, take more medication, use more medical services, and have substantially shorter life expectancies.

Doesn't that all ring true in "real life"? I know that if I don't have a reason to get up in the morning, I typically won't. If I lie in bed all day and do nothing, I feel terrible about myself, my self-esteem plummets, and my energy levels decline. If most of us did this for a long period of time too, we'd probably find ourselves financially broke—which certainly would make depression, anxiety, and self-esteem problems far worse. Purpose and hard work will fill your journey with passion.

THE POWER OF CONSISTENCY

Getting up and going to work every day is just one of many habits that will open up a world of opportunities for you— opportunities that you might not otherwise experience. The habits of self-discipline and consistency tend to do that. It's no coincidence that the most successful people in the world are usually the most rigorous in the daily habits that they practice.

> "Five a.m. is the hour when legends
> are either waking up or going to sleep."
> **—Anonymous**

New York Times reporter Charles Duhigg wrote about the science behind habit creation and reformation in his 2012 best-selling book, *The Power of Habit: Why We Do What We Do in Life and Business.* In it he describes the habit loop, which is the neurological pattern we all develop in our brains as we are establishing new habits in our lives that is made up of three separate elements: a cue, a routine, and a reward. We always start with a cue—something that prompts the brain to determine which habit to set in motion. This will involve a mental, emotional, or physical routine, which when put into practice will be rewarded. This makes it worthwhile for the person to continue that particular routine in the future and creates the habit.

Duhigg described the end game of the process this way: "The cue and reward become neurologically intertwined until a sense of craving emerges." He argues that craving is actually what is behind all habits: A certain mental, emotional, or physical routine becomes so ingrained in us that we begin to crave it when we do not complete it on a regular basis.

It is so important that we realize the power that habits can have on the success we will achieve in this life. There is a tremendous danger in "floating"—not maintaining consistency or habits. You may be reading this book and growing excited about getting in the game. And you may start out great, but starting is not finishing. It's not even maintaining—and maintenance of good habits over time is one of the greatest keys to success you will ever discover. Without it, you will completely torpedo your potential.

When I finally decided to stop focusing on what I didn't have and instead determined to get in the game, I had a coach tell me it takes forty days to establish a new habit. Let me tell you, getting up early every morning to go out and run so I could compete on the basketball court was a brutal habit to create. Why didn't I hit the snooze button or, better yet, crush that stupid alarm clock and sleep in? I had a purpose, and I set goals to achieve that purpose. Honestly, I hated it most mornings. But one day, something miraculous happened. The craving that Duhigg described happened in my life. I don't know if it was day twenty or thirty or forty, but I began to look forward to starting my morning workouts. It got to a point that a missed workout made something in me feel amiss. Did I crave it? I might be lying to say that was how I felt, but daily workouts had become a natural part of my lifestyle. It was the work habit that allowed me to achieve more than I had ever felt possible. It was the beginning of the journey that gave me the privilege of being the first person to get a full ride in Division I basketball with only one arm.

THE OLD-SCHOOL COACH
WHO CHANGED MY LIFE

I'd like to say that I discovered a self-disciplined life all on my own, but that wasn't the case. I owe a great deal of my success in basketball and in my later life to the discipline and habits that were drilled into me at military school, especially by my basketball coach there, Fletcher Arritt.

Coach Arritt is a basketball legend. He coached at Fork Union Military Academy for forty-two years before retiring, turning down more lucrative and highly coveted college coaching jobs throughout the years because he knew he could contribute more to the kids who showed up at Fork Union. If that man doesn't exemplify the virtue of self-discipline, I'm not sure who does.

Along the way, Coach Arritt earned the respect of

coaching legends like Roy Williams, Mike Krzyzewski, and Bobby Knight. I, for one, will never think of Fork Union without thinking first of Coach Arritt. I'm a big guy—6 feet, 11 inches tall and 250 pounds—and I've spent my life around big guys. But this skinny old man is still the most intimidating person I've ever met. He could drill us on the court (and off) like nobody I know to this day.

When it was first suggested that I attend Fork Union, I wasn't sold on the idea. But I had broken my leg during my senior season of basketball, and any schools that had shown interest in me had found someone else. It's not like I had a bunch of colleges to choose from to achieve my dream of playing basketball. Frankly, I was feeling sorry for myself. But I listened to what some wise advisers had to say about Fork Union. That was when I began to learn more about Coach. I was told that Coach Arritt's reputation could literally move a college coach to offer a kid a scholarship based solely on his endorsement. And the evidence backed it up. Coach had sent four hundred players on to college basketball, more than two hundred of them to Division I programs, and seven of them to the NBA. I knew then that this was a man I wanted to play for and to learn from.

Did I mention that Coach was an old-school kind of guy? A habits-and-discipline kind of guy. I still smile when I think of him. I absolutely love him. But that doesn't mean I always liked him. There were workouts during which I wondered if I had landed in hell. If it was hell, I absolutely knew who the devil was. I'm joking, of course. He was a great man. But, no question about it, he was tough on us. No excuses. No whining.

> "Champions train. Losers complain."
>
> **—Anonymous**

Everybody on the team wore jock straps and identical gear from head to toe. Every day in practice, we ran the equivalent of five to eight miles. We practiced with no fouls and no out-of-bounds calls—we just played through everything.

Coach Arritt believed that what didn't kill you made you stronger, and he made us believe it too. There were a few times when I had doubts (like when I'd vomit after a grueling workout), but he proved to us time and again that if we were willing to outwork and outlearn anyone we would face, we would win.

I won't lie to you—military school was tough. I was on the other side of the country, three thousand miles away from friends and family. It was an all-boys school with no privacy—not even any bathroom stalls. We were yelled at every day. We woke up at five o'clock in the morning and lights-out was at ten o'clock in the evening. The first thing we gave up on our first day was our cell phones. No way would we be allowed to play with a smartphone during a meal. We woke up to a trumpet playing "Reveille." We went to bed to the melancholy sound of "Taps." Free time was a privilege that was sparingly doled out and scheduled. No one needed to remind me, "Kevin, we're not in California anymore." Good thing I didn't have magic shoes that I could click together three times to go back home. I would have been there in an instant!

For nine months, it felt as though I was living the same day over and over again—like Bill Murray in *Groundhog Day* but on steroids. Of course, military school isn't supposed to be easy. It's never easy to convince a boy that he needs to grow up and become a man. And it's hard to learn discipline, especially if you've never really experienced it in your life before.

Creating winning habits and mind-sets and having the discipline to stick with them day in and day out is really one of the greatest keys to prosperity that I have ever discovered. You don't wake up one morning and suddenly discover that you're successful. It takes effort—day after day after day. But with the right habits and the discipline to see them through, practicing a lifestyle of success will become more and more natural to you.

I learned that lesson at Fork Union through the firm but loving guidance of Coach Arritt. I thought I was disciplined before, but this year of my life was when I learned it well. And it made me who I am—not just on the basketball court, but also in a successful life that I am building even to this day. Even now, if I have too much free time, I begin to wonder what I am making of my life. Have I gotten off track? Have I quit playing the game? Is there something more I can be doing to bless those around me?

"Discipline is the ability to give yourself
a command and then follow it."
—Anonymous

So many kids and adults that I talk to think I just somehow "made it" one day; they think my success was overnight and that I must be lucky to have had it fall into my lap.

Let me tell you: Success is not a onetime event that falls from the sky and lands on you. It's a series of calculated moves and decisions that allow you to sculpt the course of your life.

Consistency.

Rituals.

Habits you practice on good days and bad.

Perhaps it is waking up before the other members of your household so you can better plan and organize your day. Perhaps it is an exercise regimen or a diet program. Whatever habits you need to establish in your life—do it. The following habits are ones that have helped propel me forward.

1. PRACTICE POSITIVITY

Did you know that it can become a bad habit to think negative thoughts? It's so easy to just let the events of life on any given day suck you down. You think that nothing will ever change for the better and who you are now is all you will ever be.

Get your head in the game!

In order to achieve any degree of success, you need to practice a positive outlook on life.

You need to actively seek it out. Look for the positive spin on each situation that comes your way. Every moment that you are on this earth, every breath that has been given to you, is a new opportunity for you to learn and become better! Even if you fall down, even if you fail, get back up and do it all over again until you get it right.

Our mistakes and our failures do not have to define us; they can become truly teachable opportunities to grow if we let them. So many of us allow negativity to seep into our thoughts, which can lead us to doubt ourselves and ultimately paralyze our decision-making processes. We cannot move forward when this paralysis occurs. The truth of the matter is that everyone's journey to success is perilous, but the blueprint for success is to get up, raise your head high, and persevere.

To help maintain a positive attitude, consider the people you hang out with. Make sure that the people you surround yourself with on a day-to-day basis are positive, energetic people. As for the people who fill you with self-doubt and fear, you may need to step back a bit from those relationships.

One of the most important ways that I stay positive is through the power of appreciation. When you have a heart filled with thanksgiving, it means you are focusing on what you have rather than on what you don't have. We live in a society filled with angst over "first world problems." It's hard to be positive when your mind is focused on not having the trendiest clothes or latest gadgets. It makes you feel sorry for yourself. It robs you of the power of positivity.

If you're struggling to achieve a positive mind-set, a great activity to help you get on the right path is to simply list all the things you have to be thankful for. Even if you don't have much money, you can be rich in relationships and opportunities. Get started. Count your blessings!

2. SET LOFTY BUT REALISTIC GOALS

What is your life's purpose? Have you figured it out yet? If not, ask yourself: What am I passionate about? How can I make the world a better place?

If you've got your purpose firmly in hand, set goals to achieve that purpose. Finding out your reason for being on the planet can reveal many important clues to you about how you can best use your skills to achieve success and to help other people as well.

Set goals that not only provide direction in your life but also allow you the breathing room and the mental freedom to enjoy the journey you are on. In other words, set your goals high—be sure to realize your potential—but also keep them realistic so you don't get frustrated along the way. Life is a series of events and memories that we collect as we travel through this world with one another. Keeping that in mind helps you to expand your definition of success beyond just a corner office, lots of money, or even a sports or academic achievement you hope to attain.

3. FOCUS, FOCUS, FOCUS!

Sometimes there is nothing left to do but to just go and do it! Once you've got your purpose and goals set and visualized, your focus is what will ultimately get you there. Commit to your goals. Determine that nothing—absolutely nothing—will stand in the way of you achieving them!

Best-selling author Ramit Sethi writes about his success and how his habits helped him accomplish his goals in virtually every area of life. His determination caused him to identify what might prevent him from achieving success and devise simple solutions to overcome those obstacles. For example, when he determined that what was keeping him from getting out of bed in the morning and hitting the gym was actually the long walk from his bed to his closet to pick out his workout clothing, he devised an answer to the problem: Each night before going to bed, he laid out all his gym gear right next to the bed, within easy reach upon waking up.

With that tiny change in clothing location, his gym visit became a gym habit. He turned an excuse into a solution—and now he has killed it at the gym so often that he can consider that part of his life a success too.

I've discovered some other good habits that, since I've implemented them in my life, have helped to catapult me into success. See if you can make any of these work for you:

- Take a minute or two to breathe deeply when you're stressed.
- Pray.

- Spend quality time with your loved ones every single day.
- Ask for help when you need it.
- Cut excuses out of your life—for good.
- Stop procrastinating.
- Find three hobbies you love: one to make you money; one to keep you in shape; and one to keep you creative.
- Watch what you are putting into your mind—the TV shows, music, and books you feed on. Listen to podcasts that improve you and sharpen your skills. What you feed your mind will either lift you up or tear you down.

Success comes from self-discipline, which the late American writer and philosopher Elbert Hubbard said is "the ability to do what you should do, when you should do it, whether you feel like it or not." There are no shortcuts in life. Most of the time, your accomplishments depend on you getting out there and doing what you already know you need to do. Nothing is out of reach if you put your mind to it and want it bad enough to do the work necessary to achieve it!

════ FOR FURTHER REFLECTION ════

Have you determined your life's purpose yet? What is it?

What are the goals you need to set in order to achieve that purpose? How can you make them both ambitious and realistic?

What habits do you already have in place that can help you to meet these goals? What habits do you need to cultivate so that you can make success a reality in your life?

In what areas do you most lack self-discipline? How can you motivate yourself to change in these areas?

CHAPTER 4

QUITTING THE BLAME GAME

"It's all right to sit on your pity pot every now and again. Just be sure to flush when you are finished."

—DEBBIE MACOMBER

Self-pity had begun to define my life, and it wasn't pretty. In my sixth-grade physical education (PE) class, we had a weeklong unit on square dancing. *All jump up and never come down; swing your pretty girl round and around.* I was excited. I was going to be paired up with a girl who was my first real crush. Just as a sidenote, I went to Pleasanton Middle School, which was referred to as PMS. Our school colors were red and black. As the PMS Panthers, we got made fun of all the time by students from other schools. This toughened us up for the rigors of surviving middle school. I needed some toughening up. I just didn't think my moment of crushing defeat would take place at an old-fashioned hoedown. Life seemed awfully good based on PMS requiring all its sixth graders to learn the all-important life skill of square dancing. What could go wrong?

The time to square-dance finally came. I was ready to *big foot up and big foot down; make that big foot jar the ground.* After all, I did have big feet.

I had waited for PE class all day, and I was so completely stoked to get matched up with this girl—until the moment when she realized she would have to hold on to my nub, my missing left hand, for the duration of the dance. If you know anything about square dancing, hands get referenced in the patter more than feet do. *Allemande left with your left hand; bow to the partner, and there you stand.* I had big feet but no left hand.

Needless to say, my missing hand got awkward—and fast. I wish I could have swept her off her feet with my incredible square-dancing skills, but that is not what happened. What *actually* happened is that she went, "Ew!"—loud enough for everyone in class to hear. Her friends all laughed, and I went home from school that day brokenhearted, vowing to never love another girl again. (I refuse to share how many times I repeated that vow in subsequent years. Further aside: As a newlywed, I obviously overcame the trauma of sixth-grade heartbreak and embarrassment and said "I do" to the person who joined me at the altar.)

AFTER THE SQUARE DANCE

Nothing may have been quite so publicly dramatic as that square dance, but things like that happened all the time in my youth. My elementary and middle school years felt like one defeat after another. I speak to enough teens every year to know that school can feel like that for a lot of people for any number of reasons. It can be brutal. There's a reason the phrase *teen angst* is universally understood. But I just couldn't get past my height and my missing limb. I desperately wanted to be normal. I was spiraling into a pretty deep depression, given all the so-called strikes I had against me.

I endured that embarrassing day of school, keeping an eye on the clock and praying for the final bell to ring so that I could go home, lock myself in my bedroom, and spend hours upon hours playing Guitar Hero—with one hand. You would have thought I'd find another game! The world I knew was a cruel and ugly place filled with mean kids who made fun of me and adults who could never understand what I was feeling.

In my mind, it was all because of my missing hand, my nub that I imagined was followed by a high-powered spotlight so no one could ignore what I was missing—especially me. Turns out, I was partly right in my thought process. The world can be a mean place. But because the world was mean, to shield myself from the hurt and pain I was feeling inside, I created a nice array of defense mechanisms to keep myself from getting hurt. One of my greatest natural defense mechanisms at the time, which I somehow thought would shield me from a lot of extra grief and trouble, was to make excuses. I refused to take ownership of my life. I let a sense of unfairness dominate my emotions. Sure, I felt bad most of the time. But in my rationalization, it wasn't because of my own doing. How can you be blamed for something outside your control?

> "Nothing will work—unless you do."
> —Maya Angelou

Let's be clear. Missing part of my left arm was outside my control. It wasn't my fault. It did make things harder. It was unexpected, and it took a lot of people by surprise; a slight flinch on their part could cause me to spiral downward into a thunderstorm of anger and pain. But the problem with opening the door and entertaining a legitimate excuse is that it becomes easier to see, interpret, and explain *every* short-coming in light of the excuse. That's what I was doing. If I was irresponsible, mean, or disrespectful to the people in my life, including my mom, it wasn't my fault. It was because of my missing hand. It wasn't because of how I was handling a challenge.

Because of that, I didn't grow. I was emotionally stagnant, completely unable to cope with any of the problems that life was throwing my way. I was lousy to be around. I'm amazed by and grateful for the teachers, coaches, friends, and family that endured my moodiness.

Kevin, aren't you being a bit hard on yourself?

I'll bet many who are reading this are willing to give me a break. I did have a highly visible physical limitation. I was young. We don't expect teenagers to have the same level of self-awareness and emotional maturity as adults. Thank you for the kindness. But even though I was young, I had reached a point of real decision. Even if all my thoughts and emotions were still immature, I knew without a shadow of a doubt that something had to change if I was going to create the future I longed for. I knew I had to get in the game. That meant kicking all my excuse making out of my heart.

I wasn't being hard on myself. I wasn't lying to myself that I didn't have a physical limitation. When I said, "No more excuses," I was actually providing a great service to myself. It was the right time for me just as this very moment that your eyes are on the page is the exact right moment for you.

When I talk to people of all ages and from all walks of life, I don't see a major problem with people being too hard on themselves; I don't see an army of individuals who blame themselves for things outside their control (though some do). What I do see and hear is a loud roar of blaming others and excusing irresponsibility. I see bad decisions, rudeness, anger, and a lousy attitude toward whatever circumstances are being faced. Too many of us are carrying that lack of self-awareness and emotional maturity into our adult years because we are still playing the blame game. That's the wrong game every time.

I've already mentioned that the game of life is a journey. We don't arrive. We succeed, fail, and hopefully learn and grow each step of the way. Truth be told, there are still times when I want to blame my nub, my parents' divorce, the death of my dad, and my awkward height on some current shortcoming or failure.

I've learned and relearned that the most crippling attitude for me is self-pity. I can't let self-pity rattle around in my head by saying that my problems are the fault of something. My problems are mine. I own them. No one else gets credit for them. If I'm thinking, feeling, or doing something wrong, it's all on me. Every last bit of it.

I'm no expert on Shakespeare, but I know he got it right when Julius Caesar says to Brutus, "The fault, dear Brutus, is not in our stars, but in ourselves." Don't blame karma or destiny for where you are and what you're doing. This moment is based on the decisions, commitments, and habits *you* have made. My point is not to be harsh or say you and I have always been dealt a fair hand in life. For both of us, sometimes life sucks. My point is simple: Success and failure ultimately come from within us!

In my experience, excuses and self-pity are the absolute greatest hindrance to a lack of success in life and the biggest poison that keeps people from being able to reach their dreams and goals. Excuses will undermine your life, and they will kill off your dreams. Why? Because they prevent you from growing. They are ultimately just rationalizations of your failure.

EXCUSES DON'T EXPLAIN FAILURE— THEY DRIVE FAILURE

Ultimately, it is human nature to defend yourself when people attack you or when you are made to feel inadequate in some way. Everyone has a natural defense mechanism—the ability to justify to themselves why things are going so badly, why they are failing, or why others might be mocking them. That self-preservation instinct is a good thing. But where it goes wrong for most of us is when it becomes a habit to explain our every failure. Excuses—the practice of saying to yourself and everyone around you, "It's not my fault"—no longer justify your failure but actually become a driving force for failure.

> "When I lost my excuses, I found my results."
>
> **—Anonymous**

You let yourself off the hook for what is going on in your life. You project the blame for what has happened onto other people and don't accept responsibility for your part in the situation. You refuse to own it and learn from it.

But guess what? Failure is not the problem in this scenario. The thing about failure that most of us refuse to grasp is that it is also one of the best building blocks to success that you will ever encounter! You will never learn to succeed if you haven't learned to fail first. In my own life, I have failed more times than I can count. I've started and completely failed at two separate businesses so far in my life. Thankfully, the third time was a charm, and I run a successful company now.

I have also been conned—I've had all the money I owned at the time stolen from me in a pyramid scheme gone wrong. Yes, I got duped by a smooth-talking guy who promised to turn what money I had into millions and took everything. But I was the one who was ultimately responsible for vetting him and for my own finances. It was up to me to make them grow the right way, not in a get-rich-quick scheme.

It is absolutely ridiculous that as a middle school student I would enter a classroom to find a note in my desk calling me "One-Armed Jack" or "Captain Hook." That's just plain wrong. That's just not fair. That was not my fault. You probably haven't been given pirate nicknames, but you've had people in your life let you know how you are different from everyone else. Maybe you've been told you are stupid. Some people are seemingly committed to creating an environment in which they can make others feel awkward, miserable, or lousy about themselves. In many cases, they are projecting their own insecurities onto others to let you know how different *you* are so they feel better about themselves. That's the very definition of bullying. And unfortunately it doesn't end with our days at the playground.

It's wrong. It's not fair. And it's not your fault.

But you know what?

It's still not an excuse.

Despite being such a massive young man, I was quite reserved when I was younger. I didn't do much bullying of my own, but I was bullied—and it wasn't by the guys in my school. Most of the bullying I encountered was perpetrated by ruthless females. The girls in my class destroyed my self-confidence when I was growing up.

Since I was so far behind in so many ways, I was practically a Neanderthal in a Homo sapiens environment. I couldn't read until the second grade. I had a speech impediment; I couldn't pronounce my *L*s or my *R*s. I was pulled out of class for counseling and anger management. It got so bad that I was placed in special needs classes for a brief period of time. I was so far behind academically that I seemed stupid to everybody else—and the kids around me let me know that in no uncertain terms.

My defense mechanism kicked into high gear. I justified the way I reacted to my experiences. I coddled my failings as a student because "I'm dumb" (even though I knew I wasn't), because "my parents are divorced and I didn't do my homework because I left my book at my dad's house" (or was it my mom's house?), and because "my peers make fun of me" (which they did). The excuse-making habit progressed even further when my father was diagnosed with cancer. He was going to die and everybody knew it. It was a truly painful and emotional period of time for all of us. But I have to be honest. As hard as it is to admit, I used his illness to my advantage to get out of doing things I didn't really want to do.

I'll say it again. Getting a raw deal wasn't why I was failing. Moments of failure weren't even the problem. The problem was my mind-set that wouldn't allow me to learn from my failures and that would perpetuate a life of unfulfilled dreams.

"YOU SURE DO MAKE A LOT OF EXCUSES"

When we go through these incredibly difficult times in our lives, it can be so hard to not amplify that pain and create a way out of our normal, day-to-day responsibilities. In my own set of difficult circumstances, I found myself using my father's illness as a crutch.

"Poor me, poor me"—that was the mantra that kept running through my head. I didn't really like the way that people pitied me, but it did keep me from having to maintain the same standard that everybody else was held to—both at home and in school. It kept me securely locked in my comfort zone rather than forcing me to excel. Excuses became something that I used more often than I'd like to admit, but that's what I did when I was growing up, and it became very challenging.

It could have sentenced me to a life of misery and failure—or worse, mediocrity—but fortunately I was snapped out of it by someone who knew I had greater potential than I was admitting to myself.

> "Self-pity is easily the most destructive
> of the non-pharmaceutical narcotics;
> it is addictive, gives momentary pleasure
> and separates the victim from reality."
> —John Gardner

It wasn't until Coach McKnight finally said to me, "Kevin, even for someone who's been through so much hardship in life, you sure do make a lot of excuses," that I realized something needed to change. At his words, I fell silent. I wasn't capable of defending myself against that, because he spoke the absolute truth to me in that moment. Sometimes the truth cuts so deep that it's impossible to argue with it.

Coach was completely right; I had become a master of excuses. I got out of going to classes or doing homework by reminding teachers that my dad had died of cancer. I only had one arm, and I used that to get out of a lot of other things that everyone who did not have a disability would be held accountable for. I made sure that the people around me understood fully the hardships I was going through, and through that, I *rationalized* failure instead of *learning through* the failure and growing in the process.

Essentially, Coach McKnight's words hit me square in the face with a shovel—and I needed it. He was calling me out on my behavior. He gave me a swift kick in the butt, and it affected me in a way that changed my life. I was well on my way to becoming a failure. The constant excuses I was making had become the mud that my tires were stuck in on the road of life—a road that led to a big adventure just waiting for me.

That's what excuses are for you too: mud that will stick on your tires when you're on your way to an adventure.

I had been leaning on self-pity and excuses quite a bit to hobble my way through life. But the wakeup call from Coach was life changing. My lackadaisical attitude changed in an instant. Coach defined the consequences clearly. He said, "Kevin, I want to tell you something. I know you want to play D-I basketball. Three out of every ten thousand high school basketball players go on to play in Division I—and no one has ever done that with a disability before. And *it's not gonna happen for you*, Kevin, because you don't really want it. You are full of excuses for why you are failing, and that will keep you bogged down in failure for the rest of your life."

In the hardest times of my life, I had leaned very heavily on excuses to get me through. But that wasn't right, because it didn't resolve anything. It was true for me, and it is true for you too: If you pity yourself, you will never move forward in life. Not at all. Not one tiny bit. That's it. You have to own your circumstances. You have to own your challenges. You have to own your nub.

INSPIRE YOUR MIND

I have found that one of the fundamental ways that I can help myself rise above circumstances is through immersing my heart and mind in the stories of overcomers—people who faced hardship and came out on the other side of the valley victorious.

I'm not going to tell you what you can and can't watch or listen to or read, but I will say with full confidence that if you feed your heart and mind a steady diet of information and entertainment that is negative and lacking in hope, your struggle to escape the world of excuse making will be all the more difficult. Heck, I've found that my mood improves when I simply turn off the news for a week. Since bad news sells better than good news, the stories that get discussed most often would cause you to think the world is on the edge of disaster and collapse. Everyone is bad. Only awful things are happening. The reality that I've seen with my own two eyes is that this is a wonderful time to be alive. There are so many opportunities to learn, grow, and succeed that every one of us should feel motivated and optimistic.

I know better than to mess with people's taste in music, but let me just mention that there are a few artists I've cut from my playlist because my thoughts go in the wrong direction. Starve the negative. Focus on the positive. Turn to the stories of imperfect characters who faced incredibly difficult circumstances in life with grace and purpose. Learn how they became victorious, and apply those lessons to your life.

The most famous scientist of the twentieth century, Albert Einstein, was known for his theory of relativity. But his curious mind also had a practical philosophical bent. I love this statement on growing through positive stimulation, which many have attributed to him: "If you feed your mind as often as you feed your stomach, then you'll never have to worry about feeding your stomach or a roof over your head or clothes on your back."

Stories of overcomers from a multitude of sources, inspirational quotes, and poignant lessons from coaches and great teachers have all fed my heart and mind to achieve more than I ever dreamed possible.

I did experience my parents' divorce, my dad's passing at a young age, and having only one arm. And those were painful situations, no doubt about it. We all have our own insecurities; I just had a harder time hiding mine from other people. When I fed my mind with positive thoughts, it was a huge factor for me to move from the blame game to the success game.

I love to read great quotes. I don't always know the full story behind each quote, but there are powerful and pithy thoughts that keep me going in the right direction. I write them on notes and leave them around my house. I have a notebook full of favorite positive sayings. I want to be surrounded by thoughts that help me be better tomorrow than I am today. Frank Outlaw gave a perfect outline for what I believe:

Watch your thoughts, they become words;
watch your words, they become actions;
watch your actions, they become habits;
watch your habits, they become character;
watch your character, for it becomes your destiny.

THE NEW KEVIN

I played in a basketball game in high school against one of our rivals, Cal High. We were visitors, so the crowd was definitely on their side in our neck-and-neck game. With the clock winding down, our team was down by one. I got fouled on a shot and walked to the free throw line with a chance to take the lead. If you watch basketball, you know it is common practice for the home team fans to do everything in their power to distract and psych out the shooter. The Cal student body got loud. Real loud. I had been in this situation before, so I knew how to shut out the noise, or at least I thought I did. Someone in their fan base had come up with a particularly mean—and, I'll admit, clever—way to get under my skin in the event of this situation arising.

Almost in unison, the Cal High fans stuck their arms in their sleeves and then put them in the air and waved them around, calling out, "Nubby, nubby, nubby." Nearly four hundred kids in the stands were calling out my disability to try to get in my head and cause me to miss the free throws.

Oh man. I thought I was ready for anything. For a split second my head began to swim, and once again I found myself on the playground in the sixth grade being mocked. If I missed the shots, it wouldn't be my fault. No one should have to put up with that crap. Even if someone was trying to be clever, it was a messed-up joke. Talk about cruel.

But, ultimately, the joke was on them. I cleared my head. I performed my ritual on the free throw line. I told myself I could do it. *You've got this, Kevin.* I made both shots. In a moment of inspiration, I lifted my left arm high and waved my nub at them as I ran back down the court with a big smile on my face.

> "Every failure is a lesson. If you're not ready to fail, you're not ready to succeed."
>
> **—Anonymous**

That was the new Kevin. Not consumed with how unfair life can be. No longer hiding the thing that had gnawed at me my entire life. Instead, I was flashing it loud and proud for all the world to see. The old Kevin would have seethed and stewed, missed both shots, and then blamed the misses on Cal High's student body.

How did that change come about? How did I become the new Kevin? I had learned to own my nub, myself, and all my failures and wonderful attributes. I'd stopped playing the blame game. Now I was playing the game that mattered most: the game of living life to the fullest.

Owning your failures, your differences, your insecurities—that is the way to achieve success. But making excuses is the biggest hindrance to success. Even if your excuses seem legitimate at the time, you will never see your goals and dreams come to pass if you continue to lean on them.

OVERDO IT!

My father died at a young age. It happened a long time ago, but I still miss him. We had some great times together, but they were over too soon. I had to learn that there are no guarantees of a long life in this world. Death will come to us all. That's why I don't like the concept of a bucket list. Maybe it's just semantics, but I don't want to do things "before I die." I'd rather do things "because I'm alive and all in"! That's why I created my very own "Book of Life." It's not things to try to fit in before I pass from this world; instead, it's a list of things I am privileged and fired up to do because it makes life fuller.

Too many people just float through life, going to a nine-to-five job day after day, until some kind of cancer diagnosis or other life-threatening problem shakes them up to life. I don't quite understand why people suddenly try to live more fully when they figure out they are going to die, like the golden oldie "Live Like You Were Dying." Why wait? Why not start now?

Through my dad's example, I learned some priceless lessons on living. My dad lived by a single creed his whole life, not just when he was dying. He said it all the time, enough for all his kids to roll our eyes whenever we heard it. What was it? "Anything worth doing is worth overdoing."

That's just who my dad was. He worked nonstop, twelve-hour days after which he would come home and cook dinner for us and check his voice mail. If the neighbor needed something fixed, even if it was a creaky door to their house, he would do it without delay.

I remember one Halloween when even though my mom had custody, he decked out the entire house for us anyway. He hung a fishing pole in the gutter, attached it to a tree, and fixed up a skeleton with glowing eyes. Somehow, he rigged it so that if he flipped a certain light switch in the house, it would activate this mechanism. The skeleton would come to life and shoot down the tree at some poor kid who was coming up the street or knocking on the door for trick-or-treat. When we got back to his house from being with my mom, he had bags of candy for us—twenty or thirty bags of candy left over from trick-or-treaters who had dropped their candy and fled for fear of that skeleton! As Dad would say, anything worth doing is worth overdoing. That is what he was all about.

When he died, I took that creed to heart. You can react to negative circumstances in life or things out of your control in different ways. But I reacted to my father's death by wanting to make him proud. Instead of mourning his short life span or letting it propel me in the wrong direction, I wanted to pay tribute to him.

When I was eighteen years old, I made a vow in his honor. Part of that vow involved the creation of my "Book of Life." This was essentially a way to live. My dad couldn't live anymore, but I wanted to make him proud every day. My Book of Life is a bucket list without the dying part. It is my list of things that I want to experience. So far, I have been able to knock two things out each year. I have decided to live intentionally every year. I don't want to wake up some day and discover that the years have just blended together.

> "Falling down is not a failure. Failure comes when you stay where you have fallen."
> —Socrates

For my eighteenth birthday, I went skydiving. It was the first crazy activity in my Book of Life that I wanted to accomplish, so my best friends and I got together and jumped out of a plane. It was one of the most exhilarating and terrifying experiences of my life. It also kept me accountable to the no-excuses, no-blame commitment I'd made. I could have come up with a myriad of excuses as to why I couldn't go skydiving, but I didn't. I chose to go and do it. And I've been making those kinds of decisions ever since. Don't just do it, *overdo* it. Go for it. Don't just get by. Get in the game. Compete with all your heart, soul, and spirit.

Your level of success is determined by your reaction to the hard things that come your way in life. If you make excuses for your failings, if you make excuses for the pain and the depression, if you don't own yourself, if you react in a negative way—not only will you increase your chances of failure, but you also won't move forward.

Failure is not the issue; it's when you don't move forward after failure that your life will begin to stagnate. Excuses are the problem.

I skydived as the first item in my book of life; since then I've scuba dived the Great Barrier Reef, bungee jumped, white water rafted, and visited almost every continent in the world (don't worry—Antarctica is on the list). I've done things I never thought possible for a kid born with one arm. I knock out two big adventures a year because anything worth doing is worth overdoing. Living life is worth overdoing.

When I speak in high schools, I typically hang around for a couple of extra hours to talk one-on-one with young people who are going through hard times. One Friday night I stayed so late that the principal just gave me the key and asked me to lock up and mail it to him later. I appreciated his trust in me. I also appreciated that he understood the importance of the conversation I was having with one of his students who was going through a very dark valley. Missing dinner to talk to a young person who wasn't sure life was worth living was something worth overdoing.

I do the same thing when I speak in corporate settings. I don't leave until I've shaken hands and spoken with everyone who wants to meet and talk with me. I learned to overdo it from my dad. Excuses are a poison, but my successes have all been achieved through habit, discipline, passion—and the lack of excuses that I tolerate in my thinking and in my life. That is the greatest combination to any story of success.

FOR FURTHER REFLECTION

What's your greatest excuse? How is it holding you back? How would it make a difference in your life if you stopped using it and worked through your difficulties?

As my dad always used to say, "Anything worth doing is worth overdoing." What is worth "overdoing" for you today? How have you been compromising those things that are worth doing in your life instead of going full throttle to accomplish them?

Have you been dealt a bad hand in certain areas of life? How might self-pity about those areas be creeping in? How can you cut out self-pity while maintaining a sense of reality about your situation but also finding ways to move past it and achieve a greater level of success?

How do you define "success"? What will it take for you to reach it?

CHAPTER 5

RADICAL RESILIENCE

"Planning is what gets you moving; persistence is what keeps you going."

—CALVIN WAYMAN

Never give up."

How many times have you spoken those words or have heard them spoken to you? It's probably one of the most clichéd phrases ever uttered on the planet, especially when people don't know what to say to another person who is going through a tough time.

A cliché? For sure.

Good advice? The best!

Sometimes sayings become clichés because there is deep truth behind them. And one of the greatest truths you can ever grasp in life is this: You never know when success is right around the corner. But it is 100 percent true that you will never achieve success if you give up.

I like to call this concept of never giving up—and I mean never—*radical resilience.*

Many people don't have this quality. But all successful people do.

BOUNCE BACK HEROES

You are familiar with their stories. And for good reason.

Colonel Harland Sanders, founder of the fast-food chain Kentucky Fried Chicken (KFC), quit or was fired from a variety of jobs throughout a career that had more ups than downs. But at forty years of age, during the heart of the Great Depression, he started cooking chicken based on a "secret recipe" he had perfected. Sanders was tired of quitting and making excuses; he was ready to make his mark. But his turnaround wasn't very effective in the beginning. He cooked and served out of his living quarters, which were attached to a Shell gas station.

Despite the inauspicious setting, people raved about his signature fried chicken, and customers flocked to his make-shift restaurant. Over the next decade, he started adding more roadside gas station restaurants. But having resilience does not mean we avoid all setbacks. Eisenhower's Interstate Highway

System was good for the country's economy but not for Sanders. The interstate pulled traffic away from the Colonel's fledgling business, and he was forced to shutter not just his restaurants but the gas stations as well. He went into retirement broke, homeless, nearing the age of seventy, and sleeping in his car. But he wasn't done yet. He had tasted success—literally—and knew that he had a winning product. He tried a new business model and started approaching existing restaurants to franchise his top-secret recipe and pay him a nickel for each piece of chicken they sold.

At the age of 23 . . . J. K. Rowling was broke.
Tina Fey was working at the YMCA.
Oprah had just been fired as a TV reporter.
Walt Disney had just declared bankruptcy.
It's going to be okay!
—Source Unknown

He got rejected close to a thousand times, but he persevered and eventually landed his first franchise. Today, there are more than twenty-two thousand KFCs worldwide. The tale of Colonel Sanders and his Kentucky Fried Chicken is considered one of the greatest business success stories in part because he was dedicated to his purpose and unwilling to let age or rejection become an obstacle. It doesn't matter how young or old you are as you read these words. What matters is whether you are willing to get up again.

Legendary novelist Stephen King did—with a little bit of help. He sent his first novel, *Carrie*, to more than thirty publishers. All of them rejected it, and he threw his manuscript into the trash. His wife dug it out and made him send it to yet another publisher. Thankfully, he listened; *Carrie* has since sold four million copies.

His story is not unique. I grew up during Harry Potter mania, and the author, J. K. Rowling, was a single mother on welfare as she churned out page after page of one of the most successful series of all times. But when she started submitting it to publishers, the rejection letters came fast and furious. Five hundred million copies later—plus merchandise, theme parks, and movies—aren't you glad she didn't quit when nothing seemed to be going her way?

Super Bowl–winning quarterback Kurt Warner was never drafted into the NFL; instead, he went from team to team for tryouts. He was stocking grocery shelves when he finally got a call from the St. Louis Rams (now the Los Angeles Rams) to sign as an undrafted free agent. Thomas Edison failed in one

thousand trials before he created the first light bulb that actually worked. Walt Disney was fired by a Kansas City newspaper because he "lacked imagination and had no good ideas."
Even Michael Jordan, arguably the greatest basketball player
of all time, was cut from the varsity basketball team as a soph-
omore in high school.

There's a reason so many of these people are familiar. They
persevered. They didn't quit. If they had, you would never
have known their names. Almost any person who has become
successful has had to overcome setbacks and challenges and,
most painfully, the waiting game. Is there anything worse than
working hard and not seeing any results? Don't give up. Your
next step could be THE step.

It's not just the rich and famous I'm talking about. It's
everyday people who have been laid off at work, diagnosed
with a terrible disease, or betrayed by someone they trusted,
who have endured hundreds of rejection letters, haven't been
able to secure funding for a surefire idea, or have had business
colleagues let them down.

Radical resilience. No success happens without it.

SUPER HIGH HIGHS AND SUPER LOW LOWS

In my own life, I was feeling on top of the world during my
senior year of high school. I had managed to turn my "disability"

into a distinct advantage on the basketball court. That year, my dream to play NCAA Division I basketball seemed within reach. I was playing well and standing out, even entertaining some serious college offers.

After years of struggle and perseverance, I was finally gaining a name for myself as one of the best basketball players in San Francisco's East Bay. College scouts had graded me—even with my missing left arm—as one of the top high school basketball players in the entire country.

But my so-called disadvantage was starting to make me famous. The media had begun to show interest in this crazy-looking basketball player who had only one arm, and my story started to spread. I was even featured in the Super Bowl edition of *Sports Illustrated* that year. And then the phone rang. Right in the middle of class during my senior year of high school. I probably shouldn't have answered it, but I did.

It was the White House.

The president of the United States at that time, George W. Bush, had seen my story and been inspired. His upcoming travel schedule was bringing him to San Francisco within a few short days.

President George W. Bush wanted to meet with *me*. I was on top of the world. A few games before I was scheduled to go and shake the president's hand, I had been out on the court, and I landed oddly after a jump. My leg shifted strangely beneath me, and I felt a bit of pain, but at the time it didn't seem too severe. I shook it off and kept going—on a pretty amazing high because the *president of the United States* wanted to meet *me*.

That afternoon was amazing. My mother, my stepfather, and I were escorted out onto the tarmac at the San Francisco airport—and there it was. Air Force One. The president stepped out, and we chatted as the news cameras rolled. President Bush shook my hand and shared how proud he was of me and everything I had accomplished. It was incredible.

But sometimes our greatest highs can be followed, almost immediately, by our lowest lows. I met the president of the United States, and the very same night, I broke my leg.

As I rushed from the airport and my meeting with the president to get ready for that evening's game, traffic got a little dicey. I got to the locker room later than I should've. Because I was feeling rushed, I didn't take the time to warm up properly, and as the game began, I started to notice the pain in my leg increasing. I tried to shake it off and continued to play the game. But I was unable to finish with my teammates, and eventually I was taken to the emergency room.

I had just ended my long eventful day of meeting with the president—with a broken leg. When the doctor spoke those words that night, he didn't have to tell me what that meant. The basketball season for my senior year—the season on which I had placed all my hopes and dreams—was over. Even if there had been a Division I basketball coach in the wings who had been willing to take a chance on me and my one arm, he certainly wouldn't want me playing for him with a broken leg on top of that. Because it occurred at the height of recruiting season, this injury could not have been timed worse. I knew that all my plans had just gone up in smoke. My dreams were not going to happen the way I had hoped.

What do you do when your dreams get shot down? Do you practice radical resilience? I am a little embarrassed to tell you what I did: I went into a spiraling depression.

It is very difficult on athletes when they get injured. For me, things had just gotten far worse. I had broken my left leg, and I couldn't use a crutch on that side because of my missing left arm. I laid in bed for three weeks, and during that time I questioned pretty much everything about my life. It's easy to regress into self-pity when you hit levels of adversity that seem to come out of nowhere.

People go through divorces and deaths of family members and loved ones. These things happen all the time. No one gets a free pass in this life. A huge part of life are the hardships that we experience, but these are the things that sculpt us. For me, my broken leg was a tremendous turning point. Because my leg was broken and I couldn't use the crutches that had been provided, I couldn't even go back to school. I truly thought I was done.

I fell into a deep depression, to the point that I contemplated not even wanting to live anymore. All I had ever had as a joy in my life had been basketball, and it was now taken away from me. I couldn't see life past my pain at that point. My life had once again shrunk to my bedroom. I was back to being that one-armed, redheaded kid who hid out in his room and played video games.

Was this all that my life would be?

TURNING THINGS AROUND

Loved ones came to support me and friends came to visit, but I still continued to live out of my own head. I managed to graduate from high school at the end of that school year, but I had no place to go to college. I had committed to an arduous rehab program for my broken leg, but I was not at all convinced that it would do any good for me. My life seemed to have veered completely off track.

With the help of my high school, I was accepted to a prep school, Fork Union Military Academy in Virginia, which I attended for a year. The regimented lifestyle there helped pull me out of my downward spiral. As a military academy, they were very strict about time. Our homework time was two hours to be spent in our rooms each evening. I generally needed only thirty minutes to complete my assignments, but for the rest of that time, we were not permitted to use the restroom, speak, or fall asleep. And we needed permission from a teacher to read any book other than what were assigned to read during our classes. The only exception to this rule was the Bible.

The hardship in my life at that time drew me into faith. I sought comfort in a Bible my uncle had given me as a high school graduation present. I made it a goal of mine to read it over the course of that school year. I had a lot of questions about faith, and I wanted to try to work them out. I did that by reading the Bible—and as I did so, I fell in love with it. No matter what your background, I think faith is an important catalyst in really living your life because it encourages you to focus on the things that are bigger and longer lasting than just you. Even if you aren't a religious person, I challenge you to give it a read. The Bible is full of inspirational stories about people who refused to quit no matter what life threw at them.

As for my own life back at military school, two hours a day is a really long time if all that you are doing is staring at a wall once your homework is finished. But those two hours each day during that time in my life gave me the focus I needed to strip away all the distractions in my life and concentrate on my faith so I could get my life back on track. It gave me that radical resilience that I needed to keep pressing forward.

Eventually, my dreams returned. But even after I was later recruited to Cal Poly, my parents experienced some serious financial difficulties, and life was still a challenge. Challenges will be present for all of us every step of the way. But I discovered that what defines us as a failure or as a success is whether we hold on to our dreams and whether we withstand the struggles that we experience—whether we practice radical resilience.

Some people might think that I experienced only smooth sailing after I was accepted into a program to play Division I basketball. I didn't. Later in life, after I went on to play basketball and eventually graduate from college, I hit hard times yet again.

A documentary was coming out on my life story. People were being drawn to me because my story was reaching a great number of people. I had become an inspiration to thousands of people. As I became more famous, I became a target.

Unfortunately, many of the people who were coming my way to make me "offers I couldn't refuse" were sharks—and I didn't know it. I fell in with a certain group of gentlemen who made a lot of financial promises to me, and one of these men was a diplomat to the United Nations. This man led the pack of those who sought to take advantage of me. He worked out of the Waldorf Astoria in New York City, and when I went to visit him, I found myself getting caught up in the glamour of New York and the high rollers who seemed to appreciate me and my story.

Before long, I was conned into making an investment of $100,000 with these men. To me, that didn't seem like a lot for a guy who had been living in the Waldorf Astoria for the past three years. But that was literally all the money that I had in the world. I hadn't grown up with money, so to me, that was an astronomical amount. I trusted these men—and they betrayed me.

Their offer turned out to be a pyramid scheme.

Because of this con, I lost my apartment, and I ended up living in the basement of my ex-girlfriend's parents' house. I lost everything I had financially. I didn't have a place to live or anything to eat. I was completely broke.

Beyond that, my trust had been broken yet again. This man had taken everything I had—including my confidence and trust in other people. For a time, I couldn't even pick up the phone and talk to people because I was so distrusting of their motives. Yet again in the course of my life, I had lost myself. It wasn't until I sat down with a friend named Jeff that the tide began to turn. He was a Wall Street insurance guy, and he told me, "Kevin, you are losing yourself. Being bitter is like drinking poison and hoping the other guy will die."

> "If you get tired, learn to rest, not to quit."
> **—Banksy**

It struck me; that is *exactly* what I was doing! That is the first time I had ever heard that rather popular saying—but it was so very true for me. I was completely filled with bitterness. And I knew immediately that I had to let that go.

We all go through harsh times, and we all get played at some point or another. Every single one of us will feel like we have been completely taken advantage of at some point in life. What makes the difference between success and failure is our radical resilience—how we will come back from these challenges.

You can't always make every shot, but it matters how you get back up to the line and shoot the next one. That's what counts.

Jeff's words really changed my outlook on my life at that time. That little bit of encouragement from one great mentor was enough to change my perspective and cure a mind-set that would otherwise have been poison to my hopes and dreams.

Something so simplistic can save someone's life. I was twenty-two years old at the time. I'm twenty-eight today, and I'm now the face of a $3.5 billion-dollar company. That's a big turnaround to make in just a few short years.

NEVER, EVER GIVE IN!

On October 29, 1941, as the world was reeling from the beginnings of World War II, British prime minister Winston Churchill had the opportunity to give a speech at the very school he had attended as a boy, Harrow School just outside Central London. The words from that speech have echoed through the years and are so relevant to us in whatever trouble we find ourselves in:

> Never give in, never, never, never, never—in nothing, great or small, large or petty—never give in except to convictions of honour and good sense. Never yield to force; never yield to the apparently overwhelming might of the enemy.

Churchill loved returning to his old school and inspiring the students there, and he did so many times. But at this particular time in the history of the world when the Nazis were taking over Europe and the situation was looking bleak, his words meant more than ever to the people of Great Britain.

In October of 1941, England was feeling desperate—the Americans would not enter the war until later that year, in December, when the Japanese bombed Pearl Harbor. In fact, the people of England, Churchill's beloved country, were feeling backed into a corner as they watched country after country—Poland, France, Czechoslovakia, and so on—fall in the wake of Hitler's attempt to take over the entire continent of Europe.

But Churchill refused to give in to fear. It wasn't an option. The tables eventually turned after years of terror and bloodshed, and the Allies won the war. The rest is history—but even after a century, Churchill's words still ring true. No matter how bleak things look, never give in to fears or doubts or anything that is keeping you from success.

COACHING IN UGANDA

The summer after I graduated from college, I was invited to an event in New York City: a fundraising dinner for the Challenged Athletes Foundation, an organization that provides support to people with physical challenges who want to compete in sports.

That evening, I met a board member named Dean Roeper. As we talked about our lives and experiences, he explained to me that his daughter, who was a high school basketball player herself, had raised money to build a basketball court in a rough section of the country of Uganda—a region known as the Dark Area because of its high levels of crime and drug activity.

Her project was not that complicated. She had helped to clear out a section of the bush and replace it with pavement and paint to provide a place for kids to play basketball and have some fun. It was just one court, but hundreds of kids and adults came to play on it every day. It had become a safe place for the people of that region of Uganda to come together without having to fear the crime that otherwise surrounded them on a daily basis.

When I met Dean that evening, he told me about an upcoming trip he was planning on taking to run a camp in Uganda on that basketball court. He casually asked me if I would be interested in joining the team, and I jumped at the opportunity. Dean thought that someone with my background as a college basketball player would be a huge asset to what they were trying to do. I agreed, and his assistant booked a ticket for me right then and there.

Almost before I knew what had happened, I found myself

in Uganda. It was my first trip ever to the continent of Africa, and I was surprised and fascinated by everything I saw. We visited local markets, and I saw freshly killed meat that made the delis of our grocery stores in America look tame. But I was also struck by the more progressive elements of Ugandan society. Even though Uganda is one of the poorest countries in the world, there were still kids on motorbikes everywhere, constantly talking on their cell phones. In that way, they could have been my teenage neighbors back in California.

Out in the villages, the lifestyle of the people was more rustic. We visited friends in Uganda who lived in one- or two-room homes with dirt floors. But they seemed genuinely content, and they were certainly happy to see us. Our hosts always greeted us with big smiles. The people of Uganda taught me that when you strip away the material things in life, happiness is so much easier to achieve. The most rewarding commodity is happiness—and my new Ugandan friends seemed to understand this more than any other people I'd ever met. Certainly, they were happier than most Americans would be in their situation.

Our group was not alone at our basketball camp. The best basketball team in Uganda also used this court for their daily practices and drills. I ended up working with them as we ran the camps. The players on the Ugandan team were absolutely incredible. They ranged in age from twenty-five to thirty. Among them were several exceptional athletes, but they didn't have the basketball know-how that I did. I had probably been exposed to better coaching in high school than they had in their entire lives. Thus, I assumed a coaching role and bonded with new friends in this country so far away from home.

> "Entrepreneurs fail an average of 3.8 times
> before their final success.
> What sets the successful ones apart
> is their amazing persistence."
> —Lisa M. Amos

At the end of our stay, we decided to show a rough cut of the documentary film on my life that had just been completed. They nailed a big bedsheet onto the wall of a room to serve as a screen. That room wasn't meant to hold more than ten people, but we packed in forty. The audience included missionaries and basketball players. People were sitting on chairs, on each other's laps, and on the floor.

As the show was going on, I started to feel bad. According to my own frame of reference, I've been through a lot. I've learned from my challenges, and I've become stronger. But my new Ugandan friends had faced life-and-death hurdles on a daily basis. Their lives were challenged by poverty, disease, and hunger in ways I could not begin to fathom. Their spirit of resilience truly humbled me. Watching this film among them, I began to realize how blessed I really was.

It was quiet during most of the film. No one talked, and everyone stared intently at the screen. I was nervous that the audience was going to turn on me as they watched me complain on screen and seem so dejected about the challenges that life had dealt me. When the credits rolled, however, I was no longer worried. When I looked behind me, I saw that almost everyone had tears rolling down their faces. The basketball players stood up, one at a time, to say something about me and the film. And then their coach finally rose and said, "We needed this more than anything, Kevin. I can't express what this means to us."

The team captain, their most respected player, stood up last. He was crying, and he said to me, "Kevin, my teammates don't know this, but I have leukemia and a tumor in the back of my head. The doctors have told me to quit playing. I've even passed out on the court, and the coach told me I should quit. But you didn't quit—and *I'm* never going to quit. You have taught me that today." That was one of the greatest experiences of my life. My faith had led me to bring my humble story to the other side of the world, using it to touch a troubled life.

Kristin Armstrong, the most decorated American women's cyclist of all time, astonished the world by becoming the oldest female cyclist in history to win an Olympic medal—not to mention a *gold* medal—when she finished first in Rio de Janeiro, Brazil, in 2016—one day before her forty-third birthday. Her words are an inspiration to me to try harder, push further, and reach higher in all my life goals:

I write about the power of trying, because I want to be okay with failing. I write about generosity because I battle selfishness. I write about joy because I know sorrow. I write about faith because I almost lost mine, and I know what it is to be broken and in need of redemption. I write about gratitude because I am thankful—for all of it.

Each of us faces challenges. When you go through the hardships that you will inevitably face in life, realize that it's practice. Failures in life will make you who you are. You can't be successful without failing first. How you react to it is what defines you. Your radical resilience will make all the difference.

═══ FOR FURTHER REFLECTION ═══

As the saying goes, "Bitterness is like drinking poison and expecting the person who wronged you to die." What do you think of this statement? Do you hold bitterness in your heart toward anyone? If so, what can you do to let go of those negative feelings and avoid "drinking the poison"?

What is your typical response to challenges that oppose your dreams? Do you sink into depression, as I did? Or do you push back with radical resilience, determined to turn your failures into success?

Have you recently experienced failure or faced difficulty? What steps can you take to move past these barriers and continue to vigorously pursue your dreams?

CHAPTER 6

IT'S NOT JUST ABOUT YOU

"Life's most persistent and urgent question is this:
What are you doing for others?"

—DR. MARTIN LUTHER KING JR.

Long before I ever picked up a basketball, I fell in love with the sport of baseball, and that had a lot to do with an amazing player named Jim Abbott. Jim Abbott is best known for pitching a no-hitter for the New York Yankees in 1993, but he has also been a star pitcher for the U.S. Olympic team and the California Angels. The really incredible thing about Jim, though, is that he achieved all these things despite being born without a right hand. I think you know why he is one of my heroes!

Jim Abbott loved baseball so much that he was determined to find a way to play despite his disability. He worked hard and he worked smart to fulfill his dream. Eventually, he developed a routine in which he would deliver a pitch and immediately flip his baseball glove out from under his right arm and catch it on his left hand in a seamless motion!

That maneuver was so cool and so smooth that every Little League player who saw it tried to copy it. It didn't matter that all the other kids had two working hands—they still wanted to master that move! All the other kids I knew, however, weren't as motivated as I was, and they all gave up after a while.

Me? I worked at it day and night.

Eventually, my glove transfer was almost as good as Jim's, and despite my own missing left arm, I became an all-star baseball player in the local youth leagues in my area. Before I saw Jim Abbott and his incredible glove maneuver, I had never seen another person besides myself who had only one hand. I thought I was the only person in the world facing the particular challenges of missing an arm until I saw Jim on TV. Even though he was missing his right hand and I was missing my left arm, when I saw him, I caught the first clue that having just one arm might not necessarily keep me from living my dreams.

Then, when I was in college, I had the opportunity to meet Jim in person—and my hero did not disappoint. During our time together, Jim sat with me and engaged me with all his attention. I can see now that he knew I wasn't just another hero-worshiper or fan who followed his stats in baseball. He recognized the huge role he had played in my life, and he made sure to live up to my impression of him. I hung on to every word of our conversation. And when it was time for him to leave, he shared with me this thought, which has stayed with me since that day: "Just like I was your hero growing up," he said, "you are going to have the chance to be somebody else's hero yourself." But he also reminded me that being a hero was something I would have to earn—it was a huge responsibility.

I was as inspired that day as I have ever been in my life. I told Jim that I understood what he was saying, that I would live up to that ideal, but truthfully, on that particular day, the thought was too great for me to really grasp.

But years later, in 2013, a young basketball player at Milton High School in Georgia began to generate some buzz among college basketball scouts and coaches. He was six foot four with a smooth handle, great court vision, and the ability to slash to the basket or pull up for a jump shot.

And he only had one hand.

His name was Zach Hodskins, and by the time he graduated from high school, he had signed on to play college basketball at the University of Florida. He would be a preferred walk-on at the invitation of two-time national championship coach and former NBA point guard Billy Donovan.

Turns out, Zach told me, *I* was *his* hero.

I had paved the way for *his* success.

When I began to read the news reports about Zach's success, I started to follow him with great interest. Eventually I decided to call him up and offer my encouragement. We bonded right away, talking for more than an hour, and we continued our conversations through his entire first season as a Florida Gator. At the end of one of those phone calls, I told Zach about how much I had looked up to Jim Abbott when I was a kid. I told him how important it had been for me to have an athletic hero that I could relate to and admire. Zach agreed—and then he totally floored me. "Kevin, you were that hero for me," he said.

At that moment, my sense of responsibility toward Zach skyrocketed. Today, I love Zach like a brother, and I would do anything to help him succeed. But I also realize that my growing commitment to Zach is also the fulfillment of a promise I made, long ago, to Jim Abbott. One day, I hope that Zach will pass that same commitment on to someone else who needs a hero too. That's really what a successful life is all about.

When people turn from taking whatever they can grab out of life and begin giving back instead, they become more fulfilled and live healthier spiritual lives. It's actually called "growing up." The concept of growing up doesn't mean getting taller or getting older year by year. It means giving up the fantasy that we have been put on this planet to fulfill our own desires, live only for ourselves, or meet only our needs. It means finally coming to the realization that we were put on this earth to make a difference in the lives of other people. It means moving away from the fallacy that we *deserve* things in life and moving toward the idea that we were meant to *serve*.

THE BUTTERFLY EFFECT

"Every single thing you do matters. You have been created as one of a kind. You have been created in order to make a difference. You have within you the power to change the world."

—ANDY ANDREWS

Andy Andrews is an incredible author. One of my favorites. Several years ago, he wrote a book about something called the "butterfly effect" and how it relates to our purpose and our ability to make a difference in this world. You may have heard of the butterfly effect. The premise was used in a suspense movie starring Ashton Kutcher in 2004, when the term was growing more popular in our culture.

The idea behind it is based on a paper written by a scientist named Edward Lorenz that was presented to the New York Academy of Sciences in 1963—and Edward was literally laughed out of the room for the idea. He believed that when a butterfly flapped its wings, it set air molecules in motion that, in turn, would move other air molecules next to them. Eventually, enough air molecules would be displaced that the one flap of a butterfly's wing would actually influence the patterns of weather that people experienced—*on the other side of the globe!*

> "The ultimate level of inspiration is to show others what is possible through your actions."
> —Joel Brown

Like I said, Edward was laughed right off the stage. And for years nobody believed that this theory held any weight beyond just an interesting idea to think about.

In the mid-1990s, physics professors from several universities worked together to see if Lorenz's theory just might be a possibility. And you know what? They did prove scientifically that the butterfly effect was the real deal. It actually happened, and it was reliable. It worked every time!

So what does the flapping of a butterfly's wings mean to you and me? Well, as Andy Andrews says, "Every single thing you do matters." If the flap of a wing in Africa can indirectly cause a hurricane to take place in North America, then how much more do the things I do in my life affect those around me, those I've never met, or the entire world?

Every human being on the planet has the ability to create a ripple effect on the current population of earth dwellers today and on future generations. If you're still living and breathing, then you still have a purpose for being on earth. What kind of difference you make is up to you.

You aren't here by accident. Even if you see yourself as an ordinary person, *you* can have an extraordinary impact. In fact, you might even change the world.

CHANGING MY FOCUS

For years, my greatest dream was to play Division I basketball. And then I achieved it. I became the first player missing a limb to receive a scholarship in D-I basketball.

But dreams can be fickle. My Division I reality was not all the stuff of dreams. I certainly met a lot of special people and experienced many special moments, but I was far from a star player. I made a few quality plays, and I even started a few games—but it wasn't long before I hit a ceiling that I had never anticipated. Lined up against the very best players in the country, I realized that I was at a sharp disadvantage: I truly believed I was as athletic and as talented as they were, but I was still physically unique and limited.

While my teammates labored tirelessly in the weight room with workouts customized just for them, I was the only scholarship athlete in the school without an actual weight-lifting program. Let's get real. How many coaches and trainers have studied how to maximize what I was capable of doing? There is no chapter in the manual. There aren't professional friends to call. There aren't case studies to pore over. We all had to wing it when finding ways to help me compete at a whole new level of basketball.

It was a recipe for disillusionment, and depression started to sink in. I graduated with honors in just three years, and—with a year of athletic eligibility still remaining—considered transferring to a different school to see if my basketball dream could have a happier means of fulfillment.

And then I had a revelation.

I realized that, like many elite athletes, my focus had been slowly shifting inward—toward *my own* challenges, *my own* goals, *my own* dreams. I paused—and started to look around. Moving my focus outward completely changed my outlook. I began to examine my life, not just as a young athlete, but as a young man who could make a difference with his life outside of basketball.

> "I want to inspire people.
> I want someone to look at me and say,
> 'Because of you, I didn't give up.'"
> —Anonymous

I began to notice the hundreds of letters and messages of encouragement I received all the time from young people who were facing similar challenges, and I made an effort to answer each of them personally. I flashed back to the moments before and after each basketball game that I played—when disabled children, who had traveled great distances to come and see me play, lined up and grinned as they shook my hand or took a selfie with me. I thought about the trip to Uganda I had made with the Challenged Athletes Foundation—and how telling my story there had brought tears to the eyes of people whose lives were far, *far* more challenging than my own.

I realized that deep inside of me, there was still the little boy who had finally met his hero, Jim Abbott, and was told, "You will have the chance to become somebody else's hero, but there's a responsibility that comes with that." And the growing, maturing man I was becoming was humbled by the one-handed basketball player named Zach who looked up to *me* as *his* hero.

At that moment, I realized: *It was not about me!* It had never been about me. It was all about how I could use my story of overcoming adversity to encourage and inspire others.

The athlete in me was focused on measuring my success through points, rebounds, and blocked shots. And I thought I was a failure in the Division I league because my success in that area was not what I had hoped it would be. But the real plan for my life was not to play basketball well. I was put on this earth to share my story, to motivate other people to reach for their dreams, and to effect change for the better in this world. Basketball was my means, not my message.

The problem for nearly every human being on this planet is the same problem that I was facing. When I grew too inwardly focused, I missed out on the greater purpose for my life. Don't get me wrong; basketball was important to me, and it was the opening I needed to make a difference in other people's lives. Sometimes learning to give back involves knowing how to identify your own individual talents and using those skills to contribute to the greater good and inspire those around you.

John Wooden has said, "It's amazing how much can be accomplished when no one cares who gets the credit." If you are doing good and giving back while being overly concerned with getting the credit for those good things or receiving the glory for your "selfless" acts, then you are still acting selfishly.

It's easy to see why people do this. We all want to be popular. We all want to have our egos stroked. And we all like to win. But this aspect of life can be seen quite clearly on the basketball court: A player might be playing for himself to impress a recruiting coach or win a scholarship. But if someone is only prioritizing himself, putting himself first, the team suffers—and that player ultimately loses. If an individual player puts the team first, when the team does well, he does well too—and everybody wins together.

There is no question that I am a competitive person. I want to win. I believe in competition. I believe in testing ourselves against others to see just how far we can go. But if you want to get in the game, you need to be a part of a team. You need to care about the success of others. You do your best to play your part even if it means taking a seat on the bench; you truly win when you help others be at their best. The greatest victories are shared with your teammates.

Let me tell you about one of the most impactful moments of my life, which I touched on earlier in this book, that happened just after I agreed to play for Manhattan College. This really put things into perspective and helped me focus on others.

THE SIMPLE ACT OF TYING MY SHOES

Skip Connors was a terrific Division I basketball player in the 1980s. He was born in New Jersey, and he attended my alma mater, Manhattan College, for a year before he transferred to the University of Massachusetts and became an extremely successful student athlete there. To this day, the outstanding scholar among University of Massachusetts basketball players is honored with the Skip Connors Award.

Years later, as I was well into my own basketball career, Skip was excited about becoming a new father. His wife, Rachel, was pregnant with their second child—a boy they planned to name Jackson. The day she gave birth was one of the happiest of Skip's life—until, just after Jackson entered the world, the baby was placed in the new father's arms. He looked down to count all of the fingers and toes on his precious newborn's hands and feet—and he came up short.

Jackson had been born without a left hand.

Skip was instantly plunged into a world of shock, disappointment, fear, and depression. He could not fathom how his newborn son could ever have a "good" life, and he blamed himself for bringing Jackson into the world with such a handicap. Because of his growing depression, Skip didn't behave like a typical father would with a newborn. Instead of reaching out to his friends and family members to share his pain, he closed himself off, telling hardly anyone about his son's disability.

> "I'm a big believer in the power of one,
> that one person, one action, can have
> a ripple effect that can make a difference."
> —Gavin Armstrong

Then, one day, he saw my picture on the cover of the *New York Times*. I had "made it"—I had become a success in the eyes of the world, playing Division I basketball while missing a left hand—just like Jackson.

Skip had never heard of me before. He had heard plenty of doctors talk about his son's prognosis and what lay ahead, but this article from the *Times* reached his heart like no doctor's words ever had. I was a basketball player, an athlete—not a doctor. When Skip looked at me on the cover of the newspaper, he was also looking at his son's potential: his son's abilities rather than his disabilities. His son's future.

Not long after that, Skip discovered that I had signed a letter of intent to play at his own alma mater, Manhattan College. Skip immediately picked up the phone and called the coach at Manhattan, sobbing and asking if he could meet with me. Coach Rohrssen and Skip were old friends, so Coach invited him to the school to attend my first practice. He had told me what was going on with Jackson, Skip's son, so I was excited to meet him. After practice, I went over to Skip and shook his hand. As we stood there casually chatting, I noticed that my shoe was untied, and I knelt down to tie it without a second thought.

By the time I stood back up, Skip was weeping.

At first, I didn't understand. Then he explained, "Kevin, I really enjoyed watching you play basketball today, but forget about that. Watching you tie your shoe just now meant more to me than anything you could have said. Now I know that my son will be okay. He will be able to do whatever he sets his mind to do—and I thank you for showing me that."

The simple act of tying my shoe changed that anguished

father's perception of his baby boy. He stopped worrying about how Jackson was going to complete simple tasks and instead started to imagine all of the amazing things that Jackson could become.

It's funny to think about it now, but my grandma once told me that when I was born, everybody just assumed that I would never be able to tie my own shoes. I must have realized that somehow and taken it personally, because now whenever I speak at camps and schools, I like to challenge the kids to a shoe-tying contest. When I beat them all, it's a great way to demonstrate that we are all capable of doing things that other people say we can't do!

> "Someone is sitting in the shade today because someone else planted a tree a long time ago."
> —Warren Buffett

Today Jackson is the most adorable kid in the world, and he's crazy about basketball. It has been such a blessing to see the impact I have had on his life, and how Skip and Rachel are able to raise him as the smart, capable, independent kid he was always meant to be. As he has grown, Jackson has become a star athlete in both baseball and basketball. I hope someday he surpasses my accomplishments in the game. He certainly has the potential!

You are meant for success, but it's not all about you! You were meant to make a difference in this world, to inspire others, and to be somebody's hero.

BE THE CHANGE

"It begins with you."

—LISA CAPRETTO

You have the ability to make a difference to the people around you.

But this isn't what we typically learn from our parents, schools, coaches, or friends. From the moment we're old enough to grasp what it means, we begin to learn—both implicitly and explicitly—that "you can't change other people; you can only change yourself!" Does that sound familiar? If so, it's because it's a mantra that we have been telling ourselves and teaching our kids for years and years.

Especially when it comes to unhappy people, we learn that our attitude is the only one we can really control. If our parents are mad, we simply learn to tuck our tails and hide until the storm blows over. Teacher upset? Try to be the good student with all the right answers. Later in life—please the boss even if he won't recognize your accomplishments. If a friend gossips, don't join in, but you probably won't be able to change your friend's habits. The only one you can control is you, right?

Wrong.

> "To make a difference in someone's life,
> you don't have to be brilliant, rich, beautiful,
> or perfect. You just have to care."
> —Mandy Hale

That's basically *a lie we tell ourselves*, says one happiness researcher. Shawn Achor spent years researching the topic of happiness, even traveling to fifty different countries to study what makes positive people so successful. Achor, a Harvard graduate and a best-selling author, spoke about his findings in Oprah's *SuperSoul Sessions*, and he asserts that contrary to popular belief, it *is* possible to change the attitude of people around you.

"Happiness is an individual choice, but we are influencing people all the time," Achor says. In other words, you are the only one who controls yourself, and the same is true of other people, but we do have a strong influence on each other—and that influence can be used to make a positive impact on our world.

The strategy is to be intentional about it. Without this intentionality, if we don't watch ourselves, the negative people will rub off on us rather than the other way around. But Achor says that if you can find a way to block those negative influences from affecting your brain, you are the one who becomes incredibly powerful in the relationship. You become the influencer, not the other way around.

"If [we] find a way to . . . create a single positive behavioral change, we can watch that positive behavioral change wirelessly ripple out and tip other people's brains towards the belief that our behavior matters, towards the belief that change is possible, and that happiness could actually be a choice," he explains. It's not just about you. You were meant to change the world, to make it a better place! How can you get started today?

FOR FURTHER REFLECTION

Who are the heroes who have helped shape your own life? What qualities or characteristics did they display that meant the most to you? How is your life different as a result of their influence?

Have you ever considered the idea that you are meant to be a hero to somebody else? What opportunities do you have to give back to others in this way? How can you begin to take advantage of those opportunities in greater ways?

Have you ever heard of the butterfly effect? How can the smallest things you do have the greatest impact on those around you? How can you maximize the talents and gifts that you have been given in order to change the world?

What do you think about the idea that being a hero carries a weight of responsibility? What responsibilities might come with being an inspiration to others?

CHAPTER 7

PAY ATTENTION!

"If you truly want to change your life, you must first change your mind."

—ANONYMOUS

Get your head in the game!"

I can't tell you how many times I have heard those words from coaches over the years, and even now that I am out in the "real world," the same principle applies. It all boils down to what you, too, have probably heard all your life from parents, teachers, coaches, and maybe even whoever taught you how to drive: Pay attention!

In our crazy fast, multitasking-obsessed culture, we are often missing this essential skill called "mindfulness" by many experts. But I have found that "paying attention to paying attention" has elevated my game and brought about new levels of success—not just in Division I basketball, but also in the game of life.

BRINGING MINDFULNESS INTO REAL LIFE

When many people think of the word *mindfulness*, they tend to think of some Eastern philosophy that encourages a cross-legged yoga pose and hours of meditation to block out the world and all of its stressors. Certainly, yoga and meditation are great practices to follow, and they will surely enhance your life and allow you to reach greater thresholds of success. But that's not necessarily the kind of mindfulness I'm talking about.

I'm talking about your focus.

Your focus on your daily tasks does not need to be dictated by your environment. In other words, you do not need to carve out a completely calm, tranquil environment and peacefully empty out your mind in a quiet and comfortable setting to gain the benefits that mindfulness has to offer. Most of the time, actually, real life takes place in a noisy, messy environment, and learning how to be mindful in that environment is crucial to your ultimate level of success.

A total focus on what is going on in the present will do wonders for nearly every aspect of your life. You will reach new levels of success, and not just in your job or career—you will also see amazing results in your physical health, your emotional stability, your relationships, and even your finances.

Being present and aware of what you are doing at any given point in time brings a tremendous sense of peace. When you are actually able to focus on where you are—"in the now," as some psychologists would say—without worrying about the future, you will tap into vast internal resources you might not even know you have.

When you pay attention to what is happening in three key areas—your body, your mind, and your environment—you will find yourself able to make well-informed decisions, live more in line with your values, and practice greater authenticity in all your relationships.

PAY ATTENTION TO YOUR BODY

Have you ever noticed what happens to you when you get really stressed out? If you are anything like me, you feel it throughout your entire body.

Sweaty palms.

Butterflies in the stomach.

Clenched jaw muscles.

The start of a headache in your temples.

Sound familiar? Stress is not always the tribulation we have made it out to be in our day and age. Thousands of years ago, humans *had* to have that rush of adrenaline in their systems when they were confronted with something that was, in reality, very stressful: a predator or some other danger that threatened their survival. Thus, their instincts kicked in, and their bodies were prepared to either fight or flee. Both scenarios required a tremendous amount of energy, and so adrenaline was dumped into their systems to enable them to take the path that would best keep them alive in each precarious situation.

> "The real test of the practice of meditation
> and mindfulness is your life and how
> you conduct it from moment to moment."
> —Anonymous

These days, we don't usually need this adrenaline surge to stay alive. Most of us aren't being chased by dinosaurs on a daily basis! But we still feel the effects of stress. See if any of the items on this checklist sound familiar to you:

☐ Constantly feeling anxious or worried

☐ Feeling irritable, agitated, or easily annoyed

☐ Argumentative

☐ Constantly defensive with family or friends

☐ Restless or frenetic mind-set

☐ Disrupted sleep, waking up tired in the morning

☐ Low levels of energy throughout the day

☐ Critical of yourself or of other people

☐ Difficulty concentrating or maintaining focus

☐ Frequent headaches, even migraines

I think we can agree that even dealing with just a few of these issues would quickly kill your productivity and make it difficult to achieve even a modicum of success. Wouldn't it be great to put these problems behind you and instead start reaping the benefits of a more relaxed and focused mind-set?

Just imagine:

• Higher brain functioning

• A more balanced immune system

• Lowered blood pressure

• Lowered heart rate

• Increased awareness

• Increased attention span

• Increased clarity of thought

• Decreased anxiety levels

- Feelings of calm and connectedness to others and to the world around you

Gaining these benefits can be as simple as simply breathing in and out in any given moment, silently taking in your surroundings—even closing your eyes for a minute, if it helps you gain focus—and noticing the environment around you, how your body feels, and how your mind is responding to the stimuli you are experiencing. It is so easy that anyone can do it!

If you checked off multiple items on the list of symptoms above, I encourage you to talk with a medical professional, since I know not all stress and anxiety can by addressed with breathing techniques.

PAY ATTENTION TO YOUR MIND

Paying attention throughout the day has been known to make a difference in people's mental health for decades. It can often be a coping mechanism for some people dealing with chronic mental and emotional problems so common in our society today. Mindfulness has been found to help counter the effects of depression and anxiety while also increasing self-love and self-compassion far more than stand-alone yoga or meditation sessions. In fact, one study conducted in

2016 discovered that when compared to guided meditation and imagery courses alone, added instruction in paying attention and staying present throughout the day helped combat symptoms of depression and anxiety. Paying attention to your mental health by staying present in your circumstances allows you to better regulate your own emotions and achieve a higher degree of mental health even in the most stressful of outward circumstances.

PAY ATTENTION TO YOUR ENVIRONMENT

Have you ever sat down to complete a task only to have your mind racing in all different directions? How difficult was it to get your work done when you couldn't concentrate?

One of the greatest causes of stress and burnout on the job—or even for students who are considering dropping out of school—is an inability to concentrate on one task at a time until it is complete. When we begin to practice mindfulness in these areas, we focus on what we need to do and work toward accomplishing that task. Before we know it, we are succeeding at what we set out to do. There are a few reasons for this. Paying attention—practicing mindfulness—improves our work performance by enhancing our self-control and concentration abilities. This, in turn, increases our job satisfaction, making us want to continue working toward our goals.

TIPS FOR PAYING MORE ATTENTION TO PAYING ATTENTION

If you are anything like I used to be, you are chronically addicted to stress. You take on way too many tasks, and you try to do them all at once. That's a recipe for disaster. So how can you begin to implement this practice of paying attention into your life in practical ways that will immediately get you in the game and set you up to win?

First, make it a habit.

We all have so many bad habits—we overeat, we forget to exercise, or we binge-watch Netflix shows instead of getting to bed on time. These are the obvious ones. But what about the less obvious bad habits that we need to combat—not in our bodies or our outward behavior but in our minds?

To change your mental habits, begin to notice where your thoughts go on any given day in response to whatever circumstances come your way. Are you critical? Negative? Depressed? Begin to reset your mind throughout the day. Create a routine that mentally cleanses your thoughts of negativity and intentionally finds something positive in every situation. Retrain your brain to focus on the task at hand, block out the what-ifs, and visualize the success that will follow when the job is done well.

Dr. Amit Sood, Chair of the Mayo Mind Body Initiative,

has put together a brilliant plan to bring a different focus to each day of the week, which you can read more about in his book *The Mayo Clinic Guide to Stress-Free Living*. Try using this schedule as a template for intentional areas of focus, and notice what difference it makes in your mental health, your attitude, and, as a result, your productivity and success.

Monday: Gratitude
Find things to be thankful for all day long on Monday.

Tuesday: Compassion
Choose to make an effort to decrease the pain and suffering of all living creatures with whom you come into contact on Tuesday.

Wednesday: Acceptance
Whatever you cannot change—in yourself, in other people, in your circumstances—appreciate the good and accept the bad without trying to change anything all day long on Wednesday.

Thursday: Meaning and Purpose
Consider your ultimate purpose in life. Thursday is the day to ponder where you find meaning in your existence on this planet.

Friday: Forgiveness

Friday is a great day to consider those who may have hurt you throughout the week—and let them off the hook. Learn to forgive and clean the slates.

Saturday: Celebration

We need a day each week to remember all the joy and happiness we are currently experiencing. We have so much to be thankful for today—not what has happened in the past, and not what will happen in the future. On Saturday, celebrate what you have in the present moment.

Sunday: Reflection

Sunday's slower pace is perfect to reflect on the week and consider any lessons that could be learned or recall what was accomplished through a greater awareness and focus in your life and surroundings.

In addition to these areas of focus that you can practice throughout the week, consider the following ideas to pay better attention to your body, your mind, and the situations in which you find yourself:

- Before you go to sleep each night, create an outline

of tasks you need to complete the following day. Write it down—don't just create it in your head. You will sleep better at night and have greater focus the next day to accomplish those tasks.

- Speaking of getting enough sleep, naps are a great way to "reset" your mind and regain your focus throughout the day. Researchers have found that taking twenty-five minutes in the middle of a weekday will recharge you and help you keep your mental acuity sharp.

- Be consistent. Make mindfulness a habit. Commit to it and stick to it. Pay attention to how well you pay attention!

FOR FURTHER REFLECTION

Have you ever failed at something simply for a lack of paying attention? How might a better sense of focus on the task at hand have helped you to succeed?

Out of the three areas in which we all need to maintain our focus— body, mind, and environment—of which do you need to be more aware? Why? How could you practice a greater sense of mindfulness in this particular area?

CHAPTER 8

A GREATER PURPOSE

"Singleness of purpose is one of the chief essentials for success in life, no matter what may be one's aim."

—JOHN D. ROCKEFELLER

What were you uniquely designed to do? What is the one thing you can do that nobody else can? What is that all-important thing that you were put on this earth to accomplish?

These are some of the most important questions you can ever ask yourself. And the answers largely determine the trajectory of your life. They determine what you will set your mind to accomplish every day. They determine whether you will be a failure or a success.

THE POWER OF PASSION

As you might have gathered from my story, I had a pretty rough start in life. Truth be told, I was a bit lost until I found basketball. When I found basketball, though, I fell in love with it. I had finally found the passion that I needed in order to make my mark on the world. The basketball court became the place where I finally felt alive, recognized in a positive way, important, and appreciated. Off the court I was still somewhat of an outcast—I probably put some of that on myself—but on the court, I became everyone's favorite player. I had a whole cheering section dedicated to me. Of course, my size made me stand out. But my arm (what I was coming to realize was my secret advantage) made me the underdog. And everyone loves an underdog.

In the story of David and Goliath that we discussed in chapter 2, we see the common picture of the underdog. It's the little guy, the one who has a sling instead of a menacing spear and is wearing a tunic instead of armor. When we envision an underdog, we see David. Goliath, the big guy, is supposed to squash him. In the Star Wars movies, no one is afraid that Luke Skywalker is going to pick on Darth Vader. We cheer for members of the Rebellion to defeat the evil Empire.

I never said my life has always made sense. In high school, I was always the tallest kid on the court. In terms of size, I was Goliath. God must have a sense of humor because He definitely broke the mold with me. Despite towering others, I became the "little guy" everyone rooted for. I can't tell you how good this all felt. After a lifetime of feeling inferior, I felt special for positive reasons instead.

I was convinced that I had found my purpose in life: to be a star basketball player. My mother had always taught me that God had a greater purpose for me, but as a little kid, I didn't quite understand what that meant. As I grew older, I still didn't fully understand, but I was getting closer. I was learning. I was growing. I finally realized that basketball was not my purpose in life. Basketball was my passion, which made it a powerful tool for finding my purpose and enabling me to fulfill it.

> We don't pursue our passions. They pursue us.
> But we do pursue our purpose.

As a quick aside, let me say that you don't have to pursue your passion in life. That comes naturally. It's just what you really enjoy doing. The secret is to use your passion to pursue your purpose. If basketball had been my real purpose in life, my pursuit of meaning would already be done. I made it to D-I college basketball. But no one was going to pay me to play the game. My career ended like everyone else's athletic career; there comes a moment when someone tells you that you aren't good enough to be on the team anymore. Even Michael Jordan, Larry Bird, Kareem Abdul-Jabbar, Bill Walton, and other legends of the game arrived at that moment when they couldn't play the sport they loved at the highest level anymore.

An endeavor like basketball or a particular career path or a favorite hobby or being a public speaker or anything else we do in life can never be our purpose. Purpose is not our activities; purpose is direction.

So what was mine? And what is yours? If you want to win the game, you need to know why you are playing.

FINDING MY PURPOSE

Discovering and articulating a purpose statement in life is tough work. Sometimes our vision isn't big enough for us to identify what living life to the fullest means. Sometimes we must crumple up the sheet of paper we wrote on a couple of years earlier and start over.

I feel very blessed. It was through basketball, my passion, that I discovered my purpose. I feel like it is significant enough to last me a lifetime. I feel it has a gravitas that will allow me to create a series of goals and strategies to continue striving to fulfill it. So what was the reason I was put on this earth? *I was put here to help and be an inspiration to others, to show them that there is a better way to live than to be bogged down and held back by the challenges that we all face in life.*

Some incredible events began to happen that shined a light on what I bring to the world.

My disadvantage, the nub, had not only become a secret weapon for my success, but it had also led me to my purpose in life.

This became crystal clear to me before I even graduated high school. When I was still a junior, I got a phone call from a number I didn't recognize. When I answered, I could hear a woman sobbing on the other end of the phone line. She explained that she was a mother of a one-armed son named Sean. He was a second grader who lived in a nearby town. He wasn't doing well at all. He was discouraged and despondent, and kids at school were not taking it easy on him. I was able to let her know that I had experienced the same kinds of abuse. Unfortunately, one of Sean's classmates had taken it even further. He started a rumor that Sean's condition was contagious: If anyone touched Sean's arm, their arm would somehow magically transform to look like Sean's shriveled up arm and hand.

Needless to say, Sean had been totally shunned by the other kids around him as a result of this rumor. Nobody wanted to be his friend. They treated him like he had leprosy or a severe case of the cooties, which in the second grade was as bad as leprosy. Sean was utterly ostracized. He was barely seven years old. No one wanted to go near him or touch him at all. It got to the point that if he sat down in the classroom, kids would actually pull their desks away from him. It was the worst kind of rejection, and Sean had sunk into despair.

That's when the phone call took place.

Sean's mom was about to pull her son out of school in order to homeschool him because the situation had gotten so bad. But then she saw my story on the news, and she called my school, got ahold of my mom, and spoke to me on the phone.

Because I was only a junior, I didn't completely understand the value of what she was asking me to do. But she wanted me to come and speak to the other kids at her son's school and explain to them what this kind of disability was like and what it meant. I was happy to do it. I'm not sure my motives were entirely pure (I was excited to skip my own classes for a day), but I agreed to do it.

When I got to Sean's school a few days later, I spoke in an assembly for an hour to all the kids in kindergarten through fifth grade. I played basketball with them in the gym and showed them how I tied my shoes. Almost the entire audience was in awe of my story and how I had chosen to overcome my disability. And at the end of my speech, I brought Sean up on the stage with me, in front of his whole school. Right there in front of everyone, I signed a mini-basketball and gave it to Sean as a kind of trophy in front of his peers. It was his special day.

> "The mystery of human existence lies not in just staying alive, but in finding something to live for."
> —Fyodor Dostoyevsky

I left after the assembly, decided it had been a pretty cool day, and went home. But from there I didn't think much of Sean or his story. A week later, Sean's mom called me again— and again, she was crying. When I asked her what was wrong, she said she was actually crying from sheer joy. She shared with me that since the assembly, Sean had become the most popular kid in school—and everybody wanted one arm just like him! It meant so much to her—and to Sean—and every time he went to bed, he slept with that mini-basketball right beside him.

To be somebody's hero, someone to look up to, a way for children and families to heal, a way to teach others to embrace those around them with disabilities—that is what it suddenly became all about for me. It struck me that I was able to change the perspective of all those young kids, and I know it made an incredible impact on not only their own lives but the lives of the people they would touch as well.

We are all born different. We all have a different purpose in our lives. What's yours?

FINDING YOUR PURPOSE

It is so important to identify your purpose—that thing that you were put on this earth to do. It is very easy to be robbed of happiness in life when you do not work on what matters most to you. Here are a few of my personal suggestions to live a more meaningful life.

1. **Ask.** Ask others what they think you bring to the table. You might be surprised with their feedback on how you influence others. Something you think isn't a big deal might be an incredible encouragement to your friends. There is a tool used in business called 360-Degree Feedback. The idea is that you will get feedback from the gamut of perspectives that make up your work

world: who you work for, who you work with, who works for you, who receives your work, and everyone else you interact with. What if you took the same idea and applied it to getting feedback on who you are and hints toward your purpose? Talk to someone older than you, someone younger, some peers, and so on. No one else can tell you who you are or what your purpose is, but they can give you clues. When I ask for feedback, I always remember the importance of prayer and asking God to help strengthen and grow me through the words of others.

> "Definiteness of purpose is the starting point of all achievement."
> —Napoleon Hill

2. **Gifts.** It is not an absolute rule that we will naturally be good at the things that fulfill our purpose in life, but that will usually be the case. What are you good at? What about you seems to positively influence the people in your world? If you are lousy at making money, your purpose in life may not be philanthropy. Now, it

could be that part of your purpose is generosity, which does not require a set amount of giving. And it could be that your fortune is right around the corner. But the big idea is to not pound a square peg into a round hole. What are your gifts and talents? Your answers will be a clue to what your purpose is even if you are not ready to articulate it.

3. **Heart.** Our purpose is not just about our passion or our gifts. What of your accomplishments touches not only others but also your own heart? This is a dialogue; we look outside ourselves for clues and feedback. But don't forget to look inside. What gives you a sense that you are being who you are called to be?

4. **Big Picture.** Purpose is not the same as having goals. Goals need to be written differently. The more long-range your goal, the more general it should be (I would like to graduate from a good college). The more short-term your goal, the more specific it should be (I will look at the websites of ten colleges today). Think of purpose as your ultimate long-term goal. If you put down that it is to play professional sports, what purpose will you have left if you don't make the major leagues? It can't

be about a law degree, a medical license, or a certain amount of money. It has to be big enough that you are never done pursuing it. We mentioned Alexander the Great earlier. It seems that his purpose was to conquer the world. After he had conquered everything he laid eyes on, he was devastated. What else was there to live for? What if his purpose had been to rule the world in such a way that the lives of his citizens improved?

5. **Satisfaction.** We don't pursue our passions. They pursue us. Our ultimate goal is not happiness and satisfaction. They are by-products of living a meaningful life. But happiness and satisfaction are still good clues to what our stated purpose should be. For example, would it be better for you to start a career in something that you absolutely hate and that robs you of energy and motivation? Probably not. All work can be hard, but what kind of work invigorates and excites you? Let that help define your purpose.

6. **Find One You Like.** I'm almost afraid to add this suggestion for finding your purpose in life. I don't want you take a shortcut on the hard but satisfying work of articulating your purpose. But it's true; sometimes we

connect with a movement or organization that perfectly speaks to our heart. We love what they are about, and we want to be about the same things. There is a well-stated purpose. We read it. We like it. It speaks to us and stirs us to positive action. If this happens for you, go for it! Not all of us will be able to articulate a unique purpose, but it doesn't mean that we don't make a difference in this world. It just means there are common themes of purpose in the human experience. Someone might have already stated what you are all about better than you or I ever could.

7. **Dream Big**. A dream is not the same thing as a purpose. But it is a mental picture that can help us recognize who we are and what makes us tick. Don't have small dreams based on a small sense of self. If I had written my statement of purpose when I was in second grade, it probably would have been to survive the week without embarrassment. Believe in yourself. Speak well of yourself. Dream big dreams, and let that inform your purpose. There are a lot of motivational speakers who have said something like this, but it definitely gets my attention: "If you are going to be a bear, you might as well be a grizzly."

8. **Begin with the End in Mind.** In his best-selling business book *The 7 Habits of Highly Effective People*, Stephen Covey writes, "It's incredibly easy to get caught up in an activity trap, in the busyness of life, to work harder and harder at climbing the ladder of success only to discover it's leaning against the wrong wall. It is possible to be busy—very busy—without being very effective." His antidote is to begin with the end in mind. We need to ask ourselves if the things we focus on are really important. Having a vision for the future, a sense of direction, and a life purpose helps us live with significance. Too many people get to the end of their lives and really don't like what they did to get where they are. They didn't have a higher purpose that led them to do what really mattered.

YOU WERE MADE TO SOAR

Whatever it is that you do in life that doesn't feel like work—that should be your career goal. Most of us learn this too late in life. Most of us go into jobs because we have graduated from college and have student loans to pay off, so we take whatever job we can get to pay the bills. But that is not your passion, your purpose, or your calling. You were never meant to just get by; you were meant to soar.

Whatever risk it takes, however hard you have to work, whatever you have to do—follow your passion. That is so much more worthwhile than being trapped in a career that does not suit your gifts and talents. There should be no reason for you to dread getting up in the morning. When you tap into your passion, you will wake up each day excited and motivated to get to work, do what you were created to do, and make a difference in this world.

> "It's not enough to have lived.
> We should be determined to live for something."
> —Winston S. Churchill

If you are not passionate about what you are doing, then make a change—immediately. Take a risk. Forget about taking the easy way out. Quit wasting Monday through Friday every week. Your life will fly by too quickly as it is—don't waste it on things that don't really matter.

The greatest way to rob yourself of happiness is to trap yourself in a lifestyle that you are not passionate about. And if you are not happy, then what is success?

To me, basketball was happiness. It was my niche. But

as I have gone through all kinds of hardships in life, I have learned a great deal. And one of the key lessons has been this: Basketball might not have been my purpose, but it did give me a platform to reach others. And in reaching out to people and learning how to help them through their own challenges, I found my purpose. That is where I came to understand the reason behind all the challenges I had faced.

One of the great poets of the twentieth century, Langston Hughes, put it this way in his poem "Dreams":

Hold fast to dreams
For if dreams die
Life is a broken-winged bird
That cannot fly.

Hold fast to dreams
For when dreams go
Life is a barren field
Frozen with snow.

I have fallen in love with motivating people to change their lives. I have fallen in love with making a difference in this world. I feel like I'm soaring. That's my purpose. What's yours?

FOR FURTHER REFLECTION

Have you discovered your own purpose or calling in life? If not, how can you begin to search it out?

What is the one thing that you are most passionate about? What doesn't feel like "work" to you? How might that relate to your purpose?

It was challenging for me to learn that playing basketball was not truly my purpose—and neither was overcoming a disability. When I learned that my purpose was helping others, my life was truly transformed. Is your own purpose centered around other people? If so, how? If not, how can you focus on others more than yourself?

CHAPTER 9

GET IN THE GAME!

"I don't look back. My life only goes one way—
forward!"

—JOE DUNCAN

Most people think that attaining success in life is all about
achieving goals. I would respectfully disagree. Success, to
me, means blowing your goals completely out of the water. It
means doing something no one would ever believe was possible. It means dreaming bigger than you ever imagined—and
then dreaming even bigger than that. It means doing this in
every area of life—not just in your career, but also in your
physical health, your spiritual journey, your relationships, your
family, and every other dimension of your life.

And it all starts with getting in the game!

Many people today see me as a successful person, but whatever success I've achieved so far, I've worked very hard to gain. When I look back at where I came from, at all the challenges I've faced and the obstacles I've overcome, I'm extraordinarily grateful. I know that I have been blessed beyond measure. But I also realize that the success I've realized in my life has come about because I have put into practice all the principles I've shared with you throughout this book.

> "Have goals so big you feel uncomfortable telling small-minded people."
> —Anonymous

By turning my "nub"—my partial left arm—into an unexpected weapon that my opponents never see coming out on the basketball court, I've learned to turn my deficits into assets. I consider nothing to be out of reach; if I set my mind on something, I know that I can achieve it. I quit making excuses, I quit procrastinating, and I quit the self-pitying mentality that my partial left arm, my broken family, and my dad's cancer diagnosis had pulled me into. I took charge of my own life and destiny.

You can do the same thing. I know you can.

Although I want you to succeed in everything you do, I can't guarantee your success. *You* are the one who has to put in the hard work and effort. Only *you* can make it happen. It all starts in your attitude because your thoughts shape your actions. Believing in yourself is an absolute necessity. If you don't believe in yourself, who will?

It's time to get in the game!

ASKING THE RIGHT QUESTIONS

I grew up a short drive from Mountain View, California. You may not have ever heard of that city, but I'm sure you know the company that is headquartered there—Google. Today, as a motivational speaker, I have had the incredible opportunity to speak to the leaders of some of the world's largest and most successful companies. When I lived in New York City, I had the opportunity to work with Fortune 500 corporations, leading financial firms, and entertainment conglomerates. I've been invited to speak at some of the world's leading educational institutions. I've even addressed the United Nations. But as a kid who was raised in Silicon Valley, my first chance to speak to a team of Google executives was a *real* dream come to life. I may be a Division I basketball player, but I can channel my inner geek as well as anybody!

One of my mentors, Jerry Canning, asked me to come to Google's campus and speak to his sales teams. In addition to speaking to a room filled with professionals, I would also be addressing field teams from several remote offices through videoconferencing. When I walked up to the podium, I looked out at the faces in that room and marveled at the technological wizardry that delivered the virtual attendees into the meeting. I began to wonder if I was out of my league.

Most of the faces staring back at me were pretty close to my own age. Like many high-tech environments, Google is a company made up of young people. Their employees are among the brightest and most sought after young professionals in the entire world. Many of these Google executives had overcome higher odds than I had ever faced to become a part of this team. What in the world could I offer them from my life that they hadn't already discovered in their own journeys?

Fortunately, Jerry had done a great job of setting me up. He had shown a short clip from the documentary of my life before calling me up onto the stage. I took a deep breath and jumped in. I shared my story for about fifteen minutes before opening up the room to questions.

As soon as the dialogue began, my nerves settled. I knew I belonged—that I was there for a reason. My audience could not have been more engaged or gracious. They were generous with their compliments, but I noticed that their questions differed quite a bit from the questions I usually faced at school assemblies or other venues.

The Google executives were interested in *how*:

"How did you learn to . . . ?"

"How did you overcome . . . ?"

"How did you deal with . . . ?"

While most audiences wanted to know what famous basketball players I had faced on the court, what military school was really like, who I was dating, or even what my favorite food or kind of car is, the Google executives wanted to know *how I became a success.*

> "You don't have to be a genius or a visionary
> or even a college graduate to be successful.
> You just need a framework and a dream."
> —Michael Dell

Whether it was trying to learn how exactly I tied my shoes, worked my iPhone, or caught a pass while running a fast break, this group zeroed in on the manner in which I was able to accomplish otherwise routine tasks while missing an arm. It wasn't until after the formal presentation was over and several of us remained in the auditorium chatting that I realized why.

Google, like any other high-tech firm, is in the business of innovation. Much of its evolution begins with the idea of how to take an existing task and do it differently—and faster and better. This glimpse inside their world made me see myself as an innovator too. Obviously, my innovation is not in the world of technology, but my life has demanded that I discover new ways to do old things.

The fact of the matter is that I do tie my shoes, I do use my iPhone, and I do catch passes on fast breaks. In each of those cases, I learned how to do so by testing a myriad of methods until I finally found the right way. I live in a world that is not designed for a man with a nub, but guess what? I get along in it quite well.

Since that day, I've continually challenged myself to be an innovator. I try to apply my sense of innovation to everything that I do, and I no longer limit myself to the particular physical challenges I face. Instead, I look for new ways to motivate kids and teenagers. I search for new ways to spread my message to a wider audience. (You're reading one of those new ways right now!) I pursue new business opportunities. I look for ways to share my testimony and encourage other people to be successful in their lives too. And, just as in the game of basketball, I'm committed to doing more than sitting on the sidelines. I'm committed to getting in the game.

The Google executives shared that same commitment. Finding success in life isn't easy, and they knew it. The questions they asked showed that they were paying attention to my story and humble enough to learn from the way I overcame obstacles in my own journey. I hope you share their enthusiasm. I hope you are excited about taking the discoveries about success that I've shared in this book and putting them into practice in your own life. I hope you are ready to get in the game.

PRINCIPLES TO MAXIMIZE SUCCESS

There is a myriad of books, curricula, seminars, programs, planners, apps, and other creative resources to help you maximize success in every area of your life. For me, at my age, with my unique set of experiences, my questions have centered around how I can succeed in not just sports or finances, but also in my relationship with my wife, in friendships, in the business world, and as a motivational speaker. I've had friends recommend the Franklin Planner or other worthy tools. I have no specific recommendation other than this: use what works for you. But more importantly, ask the right questions!

Here is a list of questions I use for annual checkups and monthly and weekly planning. (I've adapted them from David Loker's "11 Essential Habits for Success" at lifehack.org.)

1. Am I doing what is most important to me?

Before you can truly move forward in any area of your life, this is the primary question you need to answer. This is the challenge of discovering and identifying your core values. It took me years to discover that basketball was one of my greatest talents and the area in which I should focus. But basketball is not a value. To identify my core values, I had to dig deeper.

To be honest, I might not have really done this—and I certainly wouldn't have done it at such a young age—if I hadn't ended up in military school. There, I was forced to dig deep and examine who I really was and where my life was heading. Some of what I learned about myself was unflattering, like the selfishness I had been cultivating and the pity parties I had been throwing over what life had dealt me. After that realization, I still had to take another step and determine what exactly I wanted to cultivate in my life. My core values became: faith, hard work, self-discipline, and positivity, to name just a few.

Knowing your values is key to your success, because your principles lay the foundation for who you will become. Albert Einstein had it right when he said, "Try not to become a person of success, but rather try to become a person of value." At first, finding your core values may seem a bit off topic when it comes to achieving success, but you have to know what you believe in before you can determine your goals. Creating goals that are in line with the values you hold is essential to sparking the motivation you will need to make those goals happen. So try it.

Take some time to sit quietly and reflect on what you value most. Pick a handful of things and write them down. Then remind yourself of your values daily, and reflect on whether you are honoring those values through the things you do.

2. What am I going to do about it?

Once you've identified and listed your values, it's time for the fun part: acting on them by setting goals and developing a specific plan. Consider the goals that you have for your life. You may have quite a few. For now, though, focus on just one goal. Make it something large enough that it will give you a sense of accomplishment when you meet it, but also be sure it aligns with your core values.

The most important thing here is how well you will be able to focus on this particular goal. The more focused you are on one goal, the more likely you are to succeed. If you spread yourself too thin, you might never complete any of your projects because they will take far too long to achieve. Believe me, multitasking is not all it's cracked up to be. Of course, we all have multiple areas of life among which we circulate every day. Work, relationships, personal finances, and a hundred other compartments in life make up the whole picture of who we are—and we need to be setting goals in each of these areas. But for now, keep your goal-setting focus on just one thing until you see it accomplished.

3. When am I going to get it done?

Okay, this doesn't sound like as much fun as the dreaming stage. But if you want to live out your values in specific ways, you have to set a timetable to accomplish steps on your path to success. You need to set a date by when you'd like to achieve your goals. This involves identifying a specific time when you are hoping to have reached the success you are striving for. Keep it realistic while not giving yourself too much time. By setting a time limit, you are making the process more real and forcing yourself to focus on it.

4. What will motivate me to move forward?

If I had not chosen to foster positivity in my life, I would have achieved a sum total of absolutely nothing. You need to choose positivity as well. Believe fully in your ability to achieve your goal. Close your eyes and visualize yourself having completed your goal in the exact time frame you set out for yourself. Don't waste your time worrying about the failures that could happen along the way. Simply remind yourself that success is inevitable if you refuse to quit.

This kind of thinking involves the belief that you're unstoppable—not that you'll never fail. Others around you may believe that you will fail, but don't let yourself be swayed by the opinions of others. Become your own greatest cheerleader. As Henry Ford once said, "Whether you think that you can, or that you can't, you are usually right." The road to success can be filled with setbacks and distractions. You have to build the right mind-set to keep rolling along, even when you encounter bumps and sharp turns.

5. What happens if I get off schedule?

What are the consequences of not keeping at it? *Consequences.* That word might seem like a real buzzkill to the positivity we were just fostering in our minds. But if you think about it, consequences are not a negative thing. They're actually motivation. If you can manage to keep yourself motivated without consequences, you are an extraordinary human being. Most of us, however, need some external motivation. Contemplating potential consequences will help you keep your eye on the prize. Not getting dessert or being grounded from TV and your smartphone may sound silly, but since we live in such a simultaneously stimulating and comfortable world, we need to intentionally delay certain gratifications until they are earned.

6. What will I do the next seven days?

Really, what are you going to do? If your answer is vague, your results will be also. John Maxwell, one of the greatest motivational speakers and authors in the world today, said this in his book *Make Today Count*: "The secret of your success is determined by your daily agenda." Break down your goals into weeklong increments, and then into each day of the week, setting up a plan to reach your overall objective.

> "It's your road, and yours alone. Others may walk it with you, but no one can walk it for you."
> —Rumi

Keep the number of tasks that you need to accomplish each day as low as you can, and focus on completing only your planned tasks for each day. If you find yourself consistently finishing tasks early, add more tasks to the list for each day. In addition to that, it's a great idea to always do the hard things on your list while your energy levels are high, which usually means doing them first . . . unless they're not your top priority. That dovetails into the next question I ask myself.

7. What are my priorities for the week?

What really has to get done today? Mark Twain once said, "If it's your job to eat a frog, it's best to do it first thing in the morning. And if it's your job to eat two frogs, it's best to eat the biggest one first." What is your "frog"—that thing you really don't want to do? That thing you'd love to put off until tomorrow? As a young athlete, it was getting up early every morning to run. That wasn't nearly as much fun as shooting hoops in the gym, but no way was I going to excel in a physically demanding sport without eating the frog of conditioning!

Prioritize the tasks in front of you. Don't always do the most urgent thing first, which we all are tempted to do. Instead, avoid the "tyranny of the urgent" and pick the most important task. By always accomplishing what's most vital, you will be making clear and measurable progress toward your goals.

Keep in mind that completing the hardest task on your list first is a surefire way of increasing your productivity. If you put it off until later in the day, your energy levels are bound to drop, and finishing the harder tasks will seem daunting and maybe even impossible. But if you start off with the hardest task when your energy levels are high, you will have the focus you need to knock it right off of your to-do list. And you will feel great about it for the rest of the day!

8. What am I pouring my heart into?

Am I willing to take a risk? Am I ready to give a little blood? Am I making myself step outside my comfort zone? If I hadn't started asking myself what I was willing to give—and challenge myself with tough tasks—I would still be stuck in my bedroom back in high school, playing Guitar Hero and going nowhere. The same is true for you: Push yourself. Get out of your comfort zone. This is the best way to learn—even if you fail—and it is the best way to make progress quickly.

If you're looking for new ideas to jump-start your life, avoiding risks will not help you at all. But keep in mind that taking risks requires a great deal of self-awareness. Try to look for ways in which you may be holding yourself back out of fear. Instead, push yourself harder to be courageous, and take that next step toward your goals.

9. What happens if I don't see immediate results?

Will you keep going even if you don't get the results you want in the timing you had planned? In other words, will you persevere even when the journey gets tough? We have already considered this character trait earlier in this book, but it is so important that it bears repeating here. You have to keep going. Failure is inevitable when you take risks, which is what you have to do in order to truly succeed. By its very definition, the desire to succeed at something means that you are risking failure.

Many people tend to give up on their dreams far too soon. Don't fall into this trap! Recall how you determined your mind-set earlier, and use that attitude to visualize your success. Know that success will happen for you. A failure is merely the opportunity for you to figure out all the details for your later success as you learn what works and what doesn't. Use your failures. Treat them as the good learning experiences that they truly are—and move forward.

10. What am I learning?

Another great quote from Albert Einstein is, "Once you stop learning, you start dying." Take time every week to sit quietly and reflect on your values, your goals, and the progress you have made so far. Where have you excelled, and where can you do better? Is everything you are doing still lining up with your core values?

Always continue to look for ways to improve. Along

those lines, never stop learning. Never consider that you have "arrived." Continue to seek out progress and innovation. Search far and wide for any knowledge or wisdom that might help you in your journey to success. Embrace any inspiration and motivation that helps you keep going. Never think that you have nothing left to learn from others.

11. Am I thankful?

Finally, one of the most important things I can impress upon you is to remain humble and to be thankful for every success you achieve or every gift that you receive. With every step along your journey, honoring the forces behind your success is a wise practice to maintain.

> "One day your heart will stop beating and
> none of your fears will matter anymore.
> What will matter is how you lived."
> —Henri Junttila

I often see professional athletes on TV thanking God after a big game. I have no problem with that at all. If you want to honor God for giving you athletic ability, it just demonstrates your humility and gratitude for the raw talent you were born with. I didn't choose the body I was given, and while I have worked hard for the success I have achieved in the sport of basketball, my inclination toward athletics certainly didn't come from me. It was a gift from God, who knew me before I was born.

I love these words (which you can find all over the internet). I have jotted down these lines and placed them in various places so I see them each day:

I'm blessed with everything I need.

I am working toward everything I want.

And most of all, I thank God for what I have.

• • •

I have had many coaches throughout my career in basketball, and now it's my turn to coach others. I've poured out my life story and my heart to you here, and I've shared with you the discoveries that I made along my own journey of success. I consider myself your coach. And I count you as one of my star players!

Throughout this book, we've been practicing our "moves"—finding our purpose, creating good habits, refusing to give up, and discovering that it's not all about us. But now

I'm thrilled to tell you that the game is about to start! I'm putting you on the court, and I'm expecting you to kill it because I know that you can.

Zig Ziglar once said, "You don't have to be great to start, but you do have to start in order to be great." Are you ready? Let's get in the game!

FOR FURTHER REFLECTION

1. Identify your core values.

What are the things that matter most to you in this life? Some of them may have jumped out to you as you read through this book. Things like self-discipline, taking responsibility for your own actions, and giving to others may have struck a chord with you. Whatever those key values are for you, list them here:

2. Pick a goal and focus on it.

What is one important yet achievable goal you can set for yourself today? In what ways can you set your focus on this goal and see it through till you have achieved it?

3. Set a deadline for your success.

What is a reasonable time frame for you to achieve this goal? Make sure to keep it realistic and plan for some delays in the process, but don't give yourself too much time or you'll procrastinate. What timeline works for your success in this area?

4. Build the right mind-set.
What fears or hesitations come to mind as you think about moving toward this particular goal? How can you push past those negative thoughts and move into a greater positive mind-set while being realistic? Remember: Success is inevitable if you refuse to quit!

5. Set consequences for missing your deadline.
What "consequences" could you set for yourself that will motivate you? You know yourself better than anyone else, and you likely know what will do the trick. Write it out here, and commit to it.

6. Plan out each day of your week.
Now comes the nitty-gritty of the plan. What do you need to do each day to make your goal happen in the amount of time you have set for yourself? Make sure to keep these plans realistic and doable, but don't forget to push yourself. You will be amazed by what you achieve when you put your mind to it.

7. Set priorities.

What are the most urgent tasks in your day? What are the most important tasks? How can you better move the urgent ones out of the way to prioritize the more vital things?

8. Take risks.

What is the riskiest thing you have ever done in your life? Were you successful in it? Why or why not? What is the riskiest thing that you face today? How can you take the lessons you have learned in your previous risk-taking endeavors and use them to move forward in your future?

9. Practice perseverance.

What failures have you experienced in your own journey to success? How have they been learning experiences for you to discover "what works" and "what doesn't work"? How did you pick yourself up and keep going?

10. Reflect and learn.

How can you remain a lifelong learner? What personal heroes can you emulate—not only famous ones, but also the teachers, coaches, and family members who have influenced your life? What lessons can you learn from them, and how can you pass on those lessons to other people?

11. Be thankful.

Who or what are the forces behind you that help you suc-ceed? What talents/inclinations have you been blessed with?

ACKNOWLEDGMENTS

I am grateful for the countless opportunities I have had to share my story with hundreds of thousands of students, business leaders, and faith-based audiences all over the world. Their response to my message and the love they've shown me is the biggest motivator to continue my mission of inspiring and elevating others.

I am honored to get to share that story in a book. It really is a continuation of my life story. I used to think I was missing something necessary to make a difference in the world, but I've since discovered that I always had everything needed to live an abundant life.

I haven't made this journey alone. It truly takes a village, and I have been blessed to have many take the time to mold me into the man I am today. Coach McKnight, Coach Arritt, Coach Collins, Coach Rohrssen, and Coach Fuca for developing me as an athlete and taking the chance on me regardless of my missing left hand. David Goldberg, Dane Blair, Julian McMahon, and Franklin Martin for helping create the *Long*

Shot documentary on my life story. And a special thanks to Charlie Loventhal for being my greatest mentor and friend.

I would like to thank the two men who served as agents and publishing coaches for me: Mark Gilroy and David Sams. We had some wonderful strategy talks and navigated the bumps and bruises that came with getting my thoughts into book form. I want to thank Jeana Ledbetter of Worthy Publishing for taking a risk on a first-time author. It meant so much that you believed in me and my message. Kyle Olund, who has been great to work with throughout the editorial process. You've always had good insights to make the book better. Thank you for all your patience! I type half the speed.

How can I not acknowledge my mother, Jodi, and step-father, Jim, for always loving and supporting me. You were there for me from the very beginning of my journey with unconditional love. My Uncle Clint for being my inspiration. My Grandmother, Judy, for simply being the best. And my father, Wayne—despite not having many years with you, I am blessed for the time we shared. I will never take lightly the gift of being loved from the moment I entered this world.

The greatest thing in my life happened while I was writing this book. I asked Brooke to marry me, and she said yes! We got married in June 2019, and I am such a blessed man to have met my soulmate. I know how much you love me because of how gracefully you took care of all the details that led up to the altar while I was grinding through another round of edits. If I drove you crazy with the extra work, you did a marvelous job of hiding it. I love you, Brooke!

ABOUT THE AUTHOR

Nearly seven feet tall, Kevin Atlas commands attention when he shows up as a speaker in schools, churches, and corporate boardrooms around the world. What makes Kevin's story so remarkable is that against all odds, he became the first player missing a limb to play NCAA Division I basketball.

Kevin weaves his story around the life lessons he gained from overcoming the loss of his left arm while in childbirth, the early death of his father, a challenging home environment, and a legion of skeptics to become one of the top high school basketball players in his home state of California and earn a scholarship to play at Manhattan College in New York City. He lives in Sacramento, California.

Kevin knows you can't win if you don't get in the game. In addition to his speaking company, he is an entrepreneur who has founded and partnered in numerous successful business launches.

For booking inquiries, visit:
KevinAtlas.com